THE SAGA OF PLIOCENE EXILE...

"JULIAN MAY HAS MADE A NEW AND FRESH MASTERWORK IN THE GENRE AND HAS IRREVOCABLY PLACED HERSELF AMONG THE GREAT OF FANTASY AND SCIENCE FICTION."
—*Isaac Asimov's Science Fiction Magazine*

"MAY SHOULD BE THE NEXT ANNE McCAFFREY."
—*Publishers Weekly*

"A RICHLY INVENTIVE SERIES."
—*Science Fiction Review*

Also by Julian May
Published by Ballantine Books:

THE SAGA OF PLIOCENE EXILE
   Vol. I: The Many-Colored Land
   Vol. II: The Golden Torc
   Vol. III: The Nonborn King
   Vol. IV: The Adversary

A
Pliocene
Companion

Julian May

A Del Rey Book

BALLANTINE BOOKS • NEW YORK

Library of Congress Catalog Card Number: 84-9124

ISBN 0-345-32290-8

This edition published by arrangement with Houghton Mifflin Company

The author is grateful for permission to quote from the following:

On Beyond Zebra, by Dr. Seuss. Copyright © 1955 by Dr. Seuss. Reprinted by permission of Random House, Inc.

"There Was Once a Puffin," by Florence Page Jaques, originally published in *Child Life*, and reprinted in *The Big Golden Book of Poetry* (New York: Golden Press, 1947)

"El Desdichado," by Gérard de Nerval, from *The Selected Writings*, translated by Geoffrey Wagner (New York: Grove Press, 1957)

Manufactured in the United States of America

First Ballantine Books Edition: May 1985

To Evan:
This is for you, "Bert Candyman."
Gaudeamus igitur, etiamsi juvenes non sumus.

And I said, "You can stop, if you want, with the Z,
Because most people stop with the Z—but not me!
In the places I go there are things that I see
That I never could spell if I stopped with the Z.
I'm telling you this 'cause you're one of my friends.
My alphabet starts where *your* alphabet ends!
. . . .

You'll be sort of surprised what there is to be found
Once you go beyond Z and start poking around."

—from *On Beyond Zebra*, Dr. Seuss

Contents

Foreward • xi

A Glossary, Name Index, and Gazetteer to the • 1
Saga of Pliocene Exile,
with Pronunciation Guide

A Chronology of the Saga • 181

The Remillard Family Tree • 191

The Ocala Rebels and Their Offspring • 195

Author's Three Original Maps • 203
of Pliocene Europe

Two Maps of Ocala Island and Vicinity • 211

The Good Ship Kyllikki • 215

The Double Ourobouros • 219

Music in My Head—Science Fiction as Opera • 223

Certain Poems Quoted in the Saga • 231

The Pliocene Wildcat Lives! • 239

Pan Books Interviews Julian May • 249

Julian May Interview • 255
by Dr. Robert A. Collins

An Interview with Julian May • 269
by Darrell Schweitzer

A Selective Bibliography • 281

Foreward

AT A RECENT World Science Fiction Convention, a distinguished writer in the field got up before an audience of several thousand readers, fans, and writers and declared that science fiction and science fact have finally converged. We live in such amazing times, he said, that there are no ideas left to speculate upon. Science fiction writers have run out of things to wonder at...

And I sat there and thought: Twaddle! And I recalled nothing so much as those smug natural scientists of the late nineteenth century who were convinced that everything that could be discovered, *had* been discovered. It's certainly true that the marvels of yesteryear may seem tame today. In the nineteen-twenties and thirties, space travel was incredible Buck Rogers stuff; in the forties we were agog at the wonders of atomic energy and computers; the fifties began a period of anthropological and social speculation; the sixties and seventies went out on a limb with ecology—and every kind of disaster scenario and dystopia conceivable. And now we are well into the eighties with science fiction more popular than it has ever been; and to me, at least, it seems that never have we had such a fund of rich speculation to draw upon. No ideas left? What world is that SF writer of little faith inhabiting? There are ideas galore both in the "hard sciences" and in psychology, sociology, and the other more human-oriented studies. And thus it will always be. Science fiction will never run out of things to wonder about until the human race ceases to use its brain.

In a way, this *Pliocene Companion* is a rebuttal to anyone who maintains that science fiction's sense of wonder has decayed. In it, and especially in the Glossary, I expand on some of the extrapolation I used in my Pliocene Quartet. My Saga is primarily a piece of entertainment and its content is fantastic—*but not necessarily fanciful*. I write science fiction, not tales of sorcery and magic; and even my most improbable-sounding plot devices have a basis in science. The Glossary, and above all the Bibliography, will give you hints and jumping-off points into the wilder regions of scientific speculation. And if you think the Pliocene Saga was strange, try some of the nonfictional conjecture that's being published nowadays—then decide for yourself whether or not all the ideas have been used up.

In addition to being an imaginative key, this *Companion* also serves as a handy guide to the admittedly Byzantine complexities of the Saga. I wrote the Pliocene Quartet in the format of a historical novel, with a cast of hundreds and politics that are rather realistic, for all their gaudy metapsychic trappings; and a historical novel demands that you immerse yourself in its world, which takes effort. Though it is possible to skim along the surface, catching the adventures and laughs on the fly, many readers have told me that they enjoyed reading the books more than once, finding something new each time. This *Companion* is particularly useful the second time around; I have tried not to give away plot elements in it . . . but let the reader be warned that it is best to read this little book *after* completing the Saga for the first time, unless you intend to use the Glossary and Name Index merely to refresh your memory when you forget who So-and-So is, who appeared briefly in *Many-Colored Land*, then popped up again in *Nonborn*.

This *Companion* shows you what Ocala Island looked like, and the schooner Kyllikki, and the weird tug-of-war machine used in the Grand Tourney. It has entries on the Pliocene rivers and other natural features, sometimes giving modern analogs. Did the jargon of metapsychology seem almost but not quite coherent the first time you read about it? Go to the Glossary, where more complete explanations of esoterica are given. Although I tried to demonstrate metapsychology at work, so that by the time you finished the fourth book you'd have a fair idea of how the higher mentalities functioned, it was not possible to do as the writers did in Hugo Gernsback's day—simply stop the action and give a lecture each time a new concept was introduced. The Glossary has many definitions and some small essays on key metapsychic speculations. The dynamic-field theory is dealt with as well as I can in the Glossary; but since I am a rotten mathematician, I fear that the explanation is thin gruel. What I'd really like is for some of the more learned among you to write and tell *me* what it's all about . . .

Other essays in the *Companion* are frankly written for fun, and the three interviews may give you some notion of the kind of person I am and why I wrote these very peculiar books in the first place.

J.M.

Glossary,
Name Index,
and Gazetteer

A Glossary, Name Index, and Gazetteer to the Saga of Pliocene Exile, with Pronunciation Guide

ABADDON (uh-BAH-dun) name applied to Marc Remillard by his human opponents during the Metapsychic Rebellion, deriving from Revelation 9:11. "They [locust-like destructive monsters] have a king ruling over them, who is the angel in charge of the abyss. His name in Hebrew is Abaddon: in Greek the name is Apollyon, meaning 'The Destroyer.'" The apocalyptic nicknames were given to Marc not only because of his threats to the Unity of the Milieu, but also because of his aloof and ruthless personality, his handsome features, and the quasi-diabolical appearance of his simulacrum when he used the cerebroenergetic enhancer during the active phase of the Rebellion. *See also* the books of the Milieu Trilogy; ADVERSARY.

ACADIE (ah-kah-DEE) a "Canadian" planet of the Human Polity; the home world of Felice Landry.

ADOR THE WART-BITER (uh-DOR) Tanu sobriquet bestowed upon the child Sharn-Ador by King Aiken-

Lugonn. A wart-biter is a robust bush cricket (Decticus verrucivorus) native to Europe and southern Britain. According to superstition, warts will disappear if bitten by this insect.

ADVERSARY   in Tanu-Firvulag legend, "one who is fated from the length of the world's age to provoke the people of Duat unto Nightfall." He was also known as the Star of Morning (cf. the third verse of the Tanu Song in *The Adversary*) after a certain red planet of baleful appearance that occasionally was visible at the Opening of the Sky ceremony on Duat. In human mythology, the Adversary is synonymous with Satan and epitomizes the evil principle; but Tanu and Firvulag do not view him in quite this light. To them, the Adversary is a more complex symbol, having aspects of *antagonist* (to the battle-religion) and *pro-voker*—one who calls forth, challenges, or excites.

AETHER (EE-th'r)   in the New Universal Field Theory of the Milieu, the mental lattices; the dynamic-field phenomenon in which mental emanations propagate. *See* Lattice; Dynamic Fields.

AFALIAH (ah-fuh-LY-uh)   a large Tanu city on the north bank of the Proto-Júcar River, not far from the neck of the Aven Peninsula. It was the administrative center of a large group of plantations, mines, and collecting enterprises scattered all over southern Spain, and the principal supply source of the Tanu capital, Muriah, before the Flood. Afaliah was governed from its foundation by Lord Celadeyr. In the Milieu, the site of Afaliah lay off Valencia, beneath the Mediterranean.

AGNES VIRGIN-MARTYR   nom d'exil of a silver-torc associate of Tony Wayland who lived in Finiah before its destruction.

AGRAYNEL (AH-gray-nel)   daughter of Mercy-Rosmar and King Thagdal, born in Goriah prior to Mercy's marriage to Aiken. Lady Morna-Ia predicted that Agraynel would become queen of the Many-Colored Land.

AIKEN-LUGONN, KING   *See* Drum, Aiken.

ALBERONN MINDEATER (ah'l-buh-RAH'n)   a hybrid High Table member who became an early supporter of Aiken over Nodonn, helping to train the upstart human for his first demonstration of martial arts and his Delbaeth Quest. Alberonn was half black, with chocolate-colored skin and blond hair; he exceeded most pureblood Tanu in physical stature. His primary metafunction was creativity and he was one of the great battle-champions. In the Flood he rescued Lady Eadnar of Rocilan and her mother-in-law, Morna-Ia. Alberonn and the widowed Eadnar later married and became co-rulers of her city. Both of them served on King Aiken-Lugonn's High Table.

ALBION (AL-bee-un)   name given to the northwestern part of Europe during the Pliocene. With the opening of the English Channel, it became the British Isles.

ALBORÁN, MOUNT (ahl-boh-RAH'n)   in the Pliocene, a volanic peak in the western Mediterranean Basin, northernmost of a small extinct chain. It is now a barren islet belonging to Spain.

ALDETOX   a chemical compound formulated in the early twenty-second century, specific against the hangover.

ALF   a Lowlife miner at Iron Maiden village; killed by Howlers.

ALGETICS (al-JEH-tix)   1. The study of pain, especially as it applies to the achievement of metapsychic operancy. 2. The punishment circuits of the docilator (q.v.).

ALGIPROTE (AL-jee-proh't) a synthetic edible protein manufactured from algae and other plants, often flavored to taste like cheese, chocolate, etc.

ALIKY'S SHAFT (ah-LEE-kee) a deep, vertical well-like passage, partly natural and partly artificial, giving access to the Water Caves of the Feldberg. It was given its final excavation and fitted with a lift mechanism by one Aliky, an engineer among the first Howler settlers of the mountain.

AL-MAHMOUD, ABDULKADIR also called A.K., an ex-Rebel of Ocala, father of Jasmin Wylie.

ALTRUISM STATUTES in Milieu jurisprudence, laws governing the ethical obligations of individuals and corporations, especially under emergency conditions.

ALUTEYN CRAFTSMASTER (AL-oo-tay'n) High Table member, First Comer, and President of the Creator Guild until his deposition by Mercy-Rosmar. He freely accepted immolation in the Great Retort, but was carried by floodwaters to the Spanish mainland. He and fellow survivors went to Calamosk, where they ousted the weak Sullivan-Tonn. Aluteyn became City-Lord and expediently promoted Aiken-Lugonn's bid for kingship. Later Aluteyn was appointed Second Creator under Queen Mercy-Rosmar, but served only briefly before his death on the Río Genil.

AMADÁN-NA-BRIONA (ah-muh-DAH'n nuh bree-OH-nuh) in Gaelic, An tAmadán Mór, or Amadán na Bruidhne, meaning "the Great Fool" or "Fool of the Fort/Fairy Mound," a fatal fool of Irish legend, whose touch meant death. Encounters with the Amadán are set down by Lady Gregory in *Visions and Beliefs in the West of Ireland*.

AMALIZAN (ah-MAH'l-ih-zan) a Tanu city near the site of the modern Castres in southern France, a center of Pliocene mining activity. Its City-Lord was Artigonn; and after him, Donal.

AMATHON (AH-muh-th'n) a Tanu coercer killed at the Fennoscandian mine.

AMBER LAKES large bodies of water in Fennoscandia, perhaps analogous to the modern Baltic Sea Region, where Howlers found precious amber and traded it to the Firvulag.

AMERGAN (AH-mur-gah'n) a President of the Creator Guild on the planet Duat, who initiated both Aluteyn and Celadeyr.

AMERIE, SISTER *See* Roccaro, Annamaria.

AMPHICYON (am-FIH-see-un) or bear-dog, genus containing large omnivorous mammals of the family Canidae, with an appearance intermediate between a bear and a dog. They had a heavy build, reaching a length of 1.5 meters or more, long stout tails, powerful limbs, and digitigrade feet. The structure of their teeth suggests that they ate plant food as well as meat. A widespread and enduring form, Amphicyon appeared in the Oligocene and lasted well into the Pontian of the Pliocene. Its fossils are found not only in Europe but also in Africa, Asia, and North America. Enormous flat-footed forms named Hemicyon and Dinocyon, placed in the family of true bears (Ursidae) by Romer, were contemporaries of the Pontian Amphicyon but much less common. Except for their larger size, they apparently had a similar appearance and habits.

ANASTASYA-BYBAR *See* Astaurova, Anastasya.

ANASTOS, DIMITRIOS dynamic-field physicist, one of Basil's Bastards. In the Milieu he was an upsilon-field generator designer for G-Dyn Cumberland.

ANATOLY, BROTHER *See* Gorchakov, Anatoly.

ANDAMATHE (AN-duh-may'th) wife to the ogre Medor.

ANDRÉ properly André Sherwoode-Laroche, a member of Ocala's second generation sent on the Monte Rosa Expedition. He was the son of Allison Sherwoode and Guy Laroche, and the mate of Irena O'Malley.

ANDUVOR DOUBLETARSE (AN-doo-vor) a Firvulag stalwart, slayer of Armida of Bardelask.

ANÉAR-IA (AH-nay-ah'r EE-uh) second wife and Queen to King Thagdal after the Tanu arrival upon Pliocene Earth. Like her predecessor, Boanda, she was able to conceive only a few children within Earth's sublethal radiation envelope, and willingly accepted death in the Great Retort. Her successor was Nontusvel.

ANÉAR THE LOVING a female member of Thagdal's High Table, a redactor of the Host of Nontusvel, who perished in the Flood.

ANGEL OF THE ABYSS a name given to Marc Remillard during the Rebellion. *See* Abaddon.

ANKET (ahn-KET) a Tanu creator on the Bardelask relief expedition.

ANVERSIAN SEA (an-VUR-see-un) an embayment of the North Atlantic lying between Albion and Fennoscandia.

AQUITAINE (AH-kee-tay'n) a "French" planet of the Human Polity.

AQUITAINE, GULF OF name given to the Pliocene Bay of Biscay.

ARIET THE SAGE (ah'r-YET) a top-ranking creator in Muriah, present at Mercy's first challenge of Aluteyn.

ARKADY *See* O'Malley, Arkady.

ARMAMENTARIUM [from the Latin "arsenal"] the roster of metafunctions that an individual can marshal, especially in aggression.

ARMIDA THE FORMIDABLE (ah'r-MEE-dah) wife to the City-Lord Daral of Bardelask and after his death, the city's ruler. She was slain defending Bardelask against Firvulag invasion. Her grandson was Ochal the Harper.

ARMORICA (ah'r-MOR-ih-kuh) name given to Breton Island and the adjacent mainland of Europe across the Pliocene Strait of Redon; equivalent to modern Brittany.

ARONN (uh-RAH-'n) a PK-creator Tanu on Monte Rosa, an associate of Bleyn.

ARTIGONN (ah'r-tih-GAH'n) City-Lord of Amalizan and son of the late sister of Minanonn. He was Second Coercer in Aiken-Lugonn's High Table until his death at the Río Genil.

ASGARD (AH's-gah'rd) a cosmop planet of the Human Polity, having a formidable mountain range named the Hlithskjalf Massif.

ASLAN in the Chronicles of Narnia by C. S. Lewis, a mystical lion who serves as a sacrificial victim and redeemer-figure.

ASSAWOMPSET (as-uh-WAH'mp-set) an "American" planet of the Human Polity, Sector Base and home of the Fourteenth Fleet, birthplace of Richard Voorhees.

ASTAUROVA, ANASTASYA (ah's-TOW-roh-vuh, ah-nah's-TAH's-yuh), called TASHA BYBAR (TAH-shah by-BAH'r) surgeon and member of the Academy of Medicine and Surgery of the planet Astrakhan. She passed into the Pliocene after her transsexual transformation, during the early days of the time-gate. She was given an honorary golden torc by the Tanu as a reward for reversing the sterilization of female time-travelers, which permitted them to be used in Tanu breeding schemes. A dancer as well as a surgeon, she had a myriad of tiny bells implanted in her flesh, the muscular control of which produced music.

ASTRAKHAN (AH-struh-kah'n) a "Russo" planet in the Human Polity.

ATV abbreviation for "all-terrain vehicle," in this Saga an amphibious craft about the size of a compact ground car, measuring about 2.2 × 1.5 × 1.5 meters. The type brought to the Pliocene by Marc Remillard was of modular design. Four ATV's could be easily linked to form a roomy "fourplex." These in turn could be assembled into larger and larger units by demounting the wheels, combining the powerplants, and modifying the structural components of the chassis. The ATV's were solar-powered, equipped with sophisticated gadgetry and weapons, and had cargo-carrying trailers. They were originally designed for the exploration of rugged terrestrial-type planets. The modular combine, an ocean-going assembly capable of making

6 knots, was 11 vehicles long, 4 wide, and (mostly) 2 high. Marc and his Rebels originally brought with them one hundred and two trailered vehicles. Hagen's caravan had fifteen fourplex units plus an eightplex freight hauler that was accidentally destroyed in the Rif Mountains.

AUBERGE DU PORTAIL (oh-BAY'rzh d'yoo poh'r-TY in Milieu pron.) in English, Inn of the Portal, Madame Guderian's establishment in the hills west of Lyon in France's Rhône River Valley, which served to disguise the time-travel operation.

AURA the visible or metaperceptible evidence of operant metafunction, ranging from genuine body luminosity (in various idiosyncratic colors) to an invisible but nonetheless detectable emanation that might be farsensed or perceived with the mind's eye. The aura can be voluntarily suppressed. It is most likely to become visible when the operant is emotionally stressed. It should be noted that the glowing armor of the Tanu is not a true visible aura manifestation. Rather, the glow results when metasensitive microbes sandwiched in the glass laminations are excited to bioluminescence by the invisible aura of the wearer. If a knight became highly excited, his natural aura might kindle and overwhelm the light of the organisms— as in the "neon" effect displayed by triumphant Hunters.

AVEN (AH-v'n) Tanu name given to the Balearic Peninsula of the Pliocene western Mediterranean region. It is interesting to compare this name to the legendary Celtic Emhain (pronounced AH-vin) and King Arthur's Avalon.

AXEL a Lowlife of Hidden Springs, prominent in the early operation of the Iron Villages, who later defected to Aiken-Lugonn and took charge of the Royal Siderurgical Establishment on Breton Island.

AYFA THE MIGHTY (AY-fuh) a Great Captain of the Firvulag, battle-champion and general of the Warrior Ogresses, who became Queen Regnant of the Little People following the Flood. She was the wife of Sharn-Mes, who became co-monarch. The couple had six children.

BAAR (bah'r)   name given to the Pliocene Proto-Garonne. In the Tanu language, it means "slow river."

BAFUT (bah-FOO't)   an "African" planet of the Human Polity.

BAGDANIAN   a special-effects technician at the Grand Tourney.

BARDELASK (BAH'r-duh-lah'sk)   a small Tanu city on the east bank of the Rhône, in the foothills of the Helvetides. Its name means "Fort Perilous." It was the first ruled by Lord Daral and later by his widow, Armida. Eventually the city was taken by Firvulag forces under Mimee of Famorel. It was an agricultural center, site of the largest brewery in the Many-Colored Land.

BARONESS, THE   nom d'exil adopted by Baronin Charlotte-Amalie von Weissenberg-Rothenstein, a pilot and member of Basil's Bastards.

BARRY *See* Dalembert, Barry.

BARSTOW a ring-hockey player of the planet Acadie, injured by Felice.

BASIL *See* Wimborne, Basil.

BASIL'S BASTARDS a group of daredevils, technicians, and pilots originally assembled by Basil Wimborne, following the Aven Exodus, for the purpose of retrieving aircraft from the Ship's Grave. Two pilots and four technicians died there in the course of testing; two more Bastards were executed when they attempted to abscond with a machine, and two others were injured in accidents. Most of the survivors took part in the Monte Rosa Expedition. A complete roster includes: Mr. Betsy, Dimitrios Anastos, Magnus Bell, Taffy Evans, Thongsa, Farhat, Pushface, Pongo Warburton, Stan Dziekonski, Phillipe, Miss Wang, Clifford, the Baroness, Bengt Sandvik, Chazz, Gideon, Aldo Manetti, Nirupam, Ookpik, Nazir, Cisco Briscoe, Seumas MacSuibhne, Derek, Sophronisba Gillis, and the six who died in testing: Gavin, Jerry-Wayne, Hillel, Shig, Viroslaw, and Gurupree.

BATTLE-COMPANY fraternal name for those Tanu and Firvulag who fought in the annual Grand Combat. It had religious as well as comradely connotations, since warriors were held to be the special elect of the Goddess of Battles.

BATTLEMASTER title given to the commander in chief of Tanu or Firvulag armed forces. The original battlemasters who came to Pliocene Earth from the Duat Galaxy were Bright Lugonn of the Tanu and Sharn the Atrocious of the Firvulag. They died in the Great Ordeal at the Ship's Grave and were succeeded by Minanonn the Proud of the Tanu and Pallol One-Eye of the Firvulag. Minanonn was deposed by Nodonn some 500 years later. Pallol was slain by Aiken Drum in the Last Grand Combat. Medor was appointed battlemaster under King Sharn and Queen Ayfa. King Aiken-Lugonn retained the title of battlemaster himself.

BATTLE-RELIGION the ancient martial faith of the planet Duat, which the ancestral Tanu and Firvulag exported to their daughter-planets, precipitating an interstellar war. This is chronicled in Brede's Tale (q.v.). When the battle-religion was proscribed in the pacified colonies, a small group of stubborn adherents on the home world attempted to touch off a symbolic Nightfall War. They were outlawed and hounded to a remote star where they hoped to fight to the death among themselves. Instead, they were taken to Earth by Brede. There the battle-religion was practiced according to immemorial custom, while an opposition Peace Faction slowly took root among the Tanu intelligentsia. Minanonn the Proud, battlemaster and heretic, attempted to give the Peace Faction legal standing during the Times of Unrest. He was defeated by Nodonn and driven into exile; but the Peace Faction continued a clandestine growth until the coming of the time-travelers. The battle-religion had no priesthood. Its principal ritual was the Grand Combat and its main tenet a glorification of the warrior's way. It may be compared to the Japanese bushido more readily than to the Western concept of a religious faith. *See also* Goddess; Grand Combat; Peace Faction.

BEAR-DOG *See* Amphicyon.

BELL, MAGNUS a physician and surgeon among Basil's Bastards.

BENGT *See* Sandvik, Bengt.

BENIAMINO (ben-yah-MEE-noh) nom d'exil of B. G. Napoli, cook and factotum at Iron Maiden village when it was besieged by Firvulag.

BENNY   a ring-hockey player on the planet Acadie who took imprudent liberties with Felice.

BETIC CORDILLERA (BAY-tik kor-dih-YER-uh)   the extensive mountain range curving around the southeastern coast of Spain and west to Gibraltar, including the Sierra Nevada. Its highest peak is Mulhacén.

BETSY, MR.   nom d'exil adopted by Dr. Merton Hudspeth, a former test pilot and research engineer with Boeing's Commercial Rhocraft Division. His chosen persona in the Pliocene was Queen Elizabeth I. He was a stalwart among Basil's Bastards.

BETTAFORCA, CAMP   base camp of the Monte Rosa Expedition, situated at the foot of the South Face, adjacent to the Gresson River. Basil named the camp for the Bettaforca Pass of Elder Earth, traversed by a footpath in milder Milieu days on the mountain.

BETULARN OF THE WHITE HAND (BEH-too-larn)   veteran battle-champion of the Firvulag and First Comer. He wore a single white-glass gauntlet with his obsidian armor.

BIG GODDESS   the Firvulag name for Monte Rosa.

BILLINGS, DR.   would-be time-traveler whose trip was aborted by the reverse translation of Madame Guderian and Claude Majewski.

BILLY   a gray-torc soldier escorting Creyn's party from Castle Gateway to Roniah.

BIOCAKE   a sweet-tasting synthetic food, largely carbohydrate, vitamins, and minerals.

BLACK CRAG   in the Pliocene, highest eminence in the Montagne Noire region of southern France. It probably lay among the Monts de Lacaune. Black Crag was the site of a splendid hunting lodge belonging to the ruler of Darask. It was given to Elizabeth as a retreat by Lady Estella-Sirone, following the Flood.

BLACK FOREST, or SCHWARZWALD   a small range lying east of the Upper Rhine. It was glaciated during the Pleistocene; during the Milieu its highest elevation was the Feldberg, 1493 meters. The range is presumed to have been higher during the Pliocene. The geology of the Black Forest is similar to that of the Vosges on the western side of the Rhine Graben.

BLACK LAKE   1. A sinister body of water in Fennoscandia. 2. An underground lake within the Feldberg.

BLACK-TORC   a fatal affliction among torced Tanu infants and children, caused by maladaptation to the mind-amplifying device. Instead of enhancing latent metafunction, the torc triggers a severe nerve inflammation, with attendant pain and mental and physical deterioration. The victim usually dies within a few weeks. Black-torc was not supposed to afflict hybrid children. Offspring of the Thagdal were also alleged to be free of the trait.

BLANCHARD, OWEN   once commander in chief of the Twelfth Fleet, the Rebel armada during the Rebellion. The veteran coercer was a frail shadow of his former self when he accompanied Cloud Remillard and her companions to Spain in search of Felice. He perished during the fight on the Río Genil.

BLASTER   a powerful photonic weapon, such as a Bosch 414, having a coherent light beam jacketed by a dynamic field. Cf. ZAPPER.

BLES FOUR-FANG (bless)   a Firvulag battle-champion present at the investment of Finiah. His illusory aspect was that of a giant venomous lizard. He was killed in the Last Grand Combat.

BLEYN THE CHAMPION (blay'n)   a hybrid High Table member and early supporter of Aiken Drum, who helped train him in martial arts. After the Flood, Bleyn lived for a time in Rocilan attempting to help his widowed sister-in-law, Eadnar, regain control of the demoralized city. When Eadnar married Alberonn and the situation stabilized, Bleyn moved with his wife Tirone Heartsinger to Goriah, where he became Aiken's chief deputy. Under Thagdal, Bleyn was a fighting specialist; under Aiken-Lugonn he was named Deputy Lord PK, Aiken retaining the presidency of that guild. Bleyn was entrusted with the formal leadership of the Monte Rosa Expedition.

BLOIS (bl'wah)   a "French" planet of the Human Polity.

BLOOD-METAL   in the Tanu language "nopar o beyn," the name given by the exotics to iron, which is poisonous to them in gross quantities. The Firvulag were generally less vulnerable than the Tanu, who might succumb even from the ingestion of iron compounds. Since both Tanu and Firvulag had blood containing hemoglobin, an iron-bearing compound, the fatal reaction is probably to be explained by some severe allergy to the concentrated metal or easily assimilable ions.

BLUE, ORION   mine foreman at Iron Maiden, later working at the Vale of Hyenas; killed by Firvulag while escorting the disgraced Tony Wayland back to Hidden Springs for trial.

BOANDA (BOH-an-duh)   first wife and Queen to Thagdal in the Duat Galaxy, and First Comer to Pliocene Earth. She died willingly in the Great Retort, as was the custom

under the battle-religion, when it became evident that she
was unable to bear children in the Many-Colored Land.
Her successor was Anéar-Ia.

BOB   a Lowlife killed by Howlers on the first iron-
seeking expedition.

BODURAGOL (boh-DOO-ruh-gul)   chief redactor at
Afaliah, who helped to heal Kuhal Earthshaker and Cloud
Remillard. Later he was appointed guild president by King
Aiken-Lugonn.

BODY-FLY   the Tanu term for levitating without a steed.
Under all but emergency conditions, it was considered by
traditionalists to be a breach of etiquette. One must note,
however, that this "tradition" can only have begun with
the domestication of chalikos by the human Iskender-
Kernonn, some fifty years before the arrival of Group
Green. Perhaps the prohibition had its roots in some Duat
custom. Like many another Tanu tradition, this one was
cheerfully violated by Aiken.

BOGLE, THE   *See* Kalipin.

BOREAL OCEAN   the name given to the Pliocene Arc-
tic Ocean, which was iceless during that epoch.

BORGHILD   name given by Isak Henning to a human-
Firvulag child he fostered, who became the mother of
Karin and grandmother of Huldah.

BORIS   a Lowlife of the Vale of Hyenas, killed by Firvulag while escorting Tony Wayland to Hidden Springs.

BORMOL (BOH'r-moh'l)   City-Lord of Roniah, a powerful coercer. He was drowned in the Flood.

BOSCH 414   *See* Blaster.

BRAZOS BEN   *See* Travis, B. B.

BREDE SHIPSPOUSE (breed), also called BREDE OF THE TWO FACES   a woman native to the planet Lene, one of the daughter-worlds of the Duat Federation. Although fully humanoid, she was one of a group of women mated to gigantic interstellar organisms called Ships. Brede was at least fourteen thousand years old. She foresaw through her imperfect metafaculty of prolepsis that the battling Tanu and Firvulag, outlawed in their own galaxy, would still play a crucial role in Duat destiny and in that of a second galaxy. She prevailed upon her Ship to carry the exotic remnant to Earth. There she encouraged the rise of the Peace Faction among the Tanu and saw in the arrival of time-traveling humanity a way of accelerating racial metapsychic operancy among her charges. Brede served as the spiritual guardian of both Tanu and Firvulag during her sojourn on Earth. Her misguided hopes for Elizabeth are detailed in *The Golden Torc*. The climax of *The Adversary* leads one to assume that Brede had remained in contact with other Ships in the Duat Galaxy before she was killed in the Flood.

BREDE'S TALE   a narrative poem recited by Fitharn Pegleg, telling how Tanu and Firvulag arrived on Earth. It has been separately published in a fine miniature edition (5.2 cm × 7 cm), bound in leather with a gilt-sterling torc affixed, and illustrated with five original pen drawings by Steve Fabian. For information write: Starmont House, Box 851, Mercer Island, Wash. 98040.

BREITHORN (BRY't-horn)   a high mountain immediately west of Monte Rosa. In Milieu times its height was 4165 meters; but it is presumed to have been above 8000 meters during the Pliocene.

BRENDAN   Mary-Dedra's child by King Thagdal, supposedly unique in being the only offspring of the monarch afflicted by black-torc. One might suspect that there were others whose existence was suppressed in the interests of preserving the royal image of genetic supremacy. Brendan's hybrid brain afforded Elizabeth a redactive advantage.

BRESSE, LAC DE (bres, lah'k d') an extensive body of water that covered the lowlands east of Dijon during Pliocene times.

BRETON ISLAND the western portion of modern Brittany, which during the Pliocene was cut off from the mainland by the Strait of Redon.

BREVON-SU-MIRIKON (BREE-vun soo MIH-rih-kun) a planet of the Poltroyan Polity.

BRINTIL (BRIN-til) female redactor at Black Crag.

BRISCOE, CISCO a technician among Basil's Bastards.

BRYAN *See* Grenfell, Bryan.

BUCK (pl. bux) the Milieu slang term for the dollar, the basic monetary unit of the Human Polity. 100 pence make a dollar. A bob is a quarter of a dollar. A centibuck is one hundred dollars, a megabuck a million, etc. Cf. CENT.

BUCKMASTER, CHARISSE ex-Rebel of Ocala, the mother of Quinn, known as an expert chef in addition to her military qualifications.

BUCKMASTER, QUINN a member of Ocala's second generation, son of Charisse Buckmaster and Quinn Fitzpatrick.

BUKIN THE ESTIMABLE (BOO-kin) a Howler, head couturier at Nionel, who designed Katlinel's gown for the Grand Tourney.

BUNONE WARTEACHER (boo-NOH'n) the greatest female warrior of the Tanu under King Thagdal, a battle-champion, member of the High Table, and instructor in martial arts. She became an adherent of Aiken Drum.

BURASK (boo-RAH'sk) a small Tanu city on the Upper Nonol River west of the Lac de Bresse, along the Western Track to Goriah. Its name means "Fort Defiance." After the Flood, Burask was taken by the Firvulag. Its ruler, Osgeyr, and most of the populace were massacred, and a large arms cache from the city was seized by the Firvulag.

BURKE, PEOPEO MOXMOX, MR. JUSTICE called Chief, the last living member of the Wallawalla Indian Nation and onetime justice of the Washington State (USA) Supreme Court. The Wallawalla, whose name means "Little River," were a people of the Shahaptian linguistic group who lived along the eastern Columbia and Snake rivers and were concentrated near their eponymous river in Washington. By the late twentieth century their numbers had dwindled to a few hundred. Chief Burke's first name is the same as that of a noted Wallawalla tribal leader of the nineteenth century, whose portrait by Paul Kane can be seen in the Royal Ontario Museum. His name may mean "meadowlark." Burke served as Freeleader of the Vosges Lowlives prior to the arrival of Madame Guderian, then headed the village defense force as warlord in chief, and was a member of the Hidden Springs Steering Committee. His adventures are detailed in the four books of the Saga. In his younger days as a beginning lawyer, Burke worked in the offices of Mermelstein & Olson, attorneys in Salt Lake City. Olson, a Latter Day Saint, acquainted Burke with the Mormon belief that Native Americans are descendants of the Lost Tribes of Israel. The puckish Mermelstein instructed young Burke in Yiddish just in case this belief turned out to be true. (Variations on this comic theme can be noted in works by other writers, and are familiar to the general public from the films *Cat Ballou* and *Blazing Saddles*.)

BYBAR   *See* Astaurova, Anastasya.

CAIR PARAVEL   in the books by C. S. Lewis, the royal city of Narnia.

CALAMOSK (KAL-uh-maw'sk)   a small Tanu city on the River Ybaar in Spain. The name means "wilderness stronghold." During Thagdal's reign its City-Lord was Onedan Trumpeter, father of Olone. After Onedan drowned in the Flood, Calamosk was briefly ruled by Olone's elderly human fiancé, Sullivan-Tonn. He was deposed by Aluteyn and his band of desperados. Upon Aluteyn's death, Parthol Swiftfoot became City-Lord, and eventually served on Aiken's High Table.

CALEDONIA   a "Scottish" planet of the Human Polity, birthplace of Dorothea Macdonald and scene of her prodigious metapsychic triumph. The detailed history of this human colony is told in the second volume of the Milieu Trilogy, *Diamond Mask*.

CALISTRO   goat-boy at Hidden Springs. Children were very rare among the Lowlives—first, because of the preponderance of male over female time-travelers; second, because all females were routinely sterilized before passing into the Pliocene. Women enslaved by the Tanu who were considered "presentable" had the sterilization reversed and were impressed into breeding schemes. A fertile woman was valued Tanu property, and giving birth to a human child was grounds for execution of mother, father, and child. Apparently very few fertile women managed to escape their exotic captors and join the Lowlives, which accounts not only for the paucity of Lowlife offspring, but also for the overwhelming percentage of males among the outlaws.

CANDYMAN, BERT, nickname of **ETHELBERT ANKETELL MILLEDGE-WEXLER,** dubbed **WEX-VELITOKAL** (vel-IH-toh-kah'l)   by the Tanu. He was a silver-torc in Rocilan. Although lacking in significant latencies, he was a talented organic chemist, placed in charge of the big candy factory that was one of the principal industries of the city. He was brought to Goriah by Aiken in order to free the castle's arms cache from poisonous foam.

CAPTAL (KAP-tah'l)   a petty officer in the Tanu human forces, roughly equivalent to a top sergeant.

CARRIER   a mental impulse that can be modulated into farsent communication. A carrier can be either natural or mechanically augmented.

CARTIER, LUCILLE (kah'r-t'YAY)   grandmother of Marc and Jon Remillard; research psychologist at Dartmouth College, New Hampshire. A natural operant metapsychic, she and her husband Denis Remillard founded the Department of Metapsychology at the school and were the initiators of the Great Intervention. Their seven operant children were known as the Remillard Dynasty. Lucille's history is detailed in the Milieu Trilogy. *See also* "The Remillard Family Tree" in this *Companion*, and Intervention, Great.

CARVALHO, PETE   a technician brought along on the Río Genil expedition in order to help repair the Spear of Lugonn.

CARNYX (KAH'r-nicks), pl. carnices (KAH'r-nih-sees)   an animal-headed trumpet, usually coiled or curved. They were used not only by the Tanu, who made them of glass, but also by the ancient Celts, who utilized metal.

CASTELLANE, PATRICIA (KAS-tel-ayn)   former dirigent of Okanagon and magnate of the Concilium, one of the earliest supporters of Marc Remillard's Metapsychic Rebellion. Her primary metafaculties were creativity, coercion, and redaction. On Ocala, she was Marc's lover for most of their Pliocene exile.

CASTLE GATEWAY   a Tanu fortress built immediately adjacent to the time-gate site. After the devastation of Finiah it was used to house refugees from that city. When the time-gate was closed by Madame Guderian and Claude Majewski, the castle's use as a receiving center for human exiles ended, and it was left with only a token caretaking force. This made it vulnerable to a Firvulag attack during the Postdiluvium, which severely damaged the interior appointments. The time-gate leading from the Pliocene to the Milieu was built inside the castle, in its central courtyard.

CASTLE OF GLASS   the spectacular citadel of Goriah, originally the headquarters of Nodonn Battlemaster. During the Postdiluvium it was taken over by Aiken-Lugonn; and when he became king it served as his royal residence and seat of power. The castle was unique in the Many-Colored Land in being constructed of glass bricks and adorned with many glass structural elements. Gold lustre-work and faceted buttresses caused the structure to glitter in sunlight. At night internal illumination made it a beacon visible for many kilometers. Under Nodonn it shone a halide rosy gold. Aiken replaced these colors with his own violet and gold. The commanding eminence above the Strait of Redon where the castle once stood today forms the height of Belle Île, off the coast of Brittany.

CATALAN GULF   an arm of the Great Lagoon (and later of the New Sea) north of the Aven Peninsula.

CATALAN WILDERNESS   a wild portion of northeastern Koneyn above the Ybaar River. It was the original exile retreat of Minanonn the Heretic before he set up his stronghold in the Flaming Mountains. Later, the exiled Leyr and his followers lived there.

CELADEYR (SEL-uh-day'r)   First Comer and City-Lord of Afaliah. A stalwart of the Creator Guild, he was field-promoted to the High Table during the Last Grand Combat. He survived the Flood and gathered the remnant of Nontusvel's Host and other Tanu conservatives under his aegis, in order to resist Aiken's usurpation of the Tanu throne. Celadeyr was a principal in the abortive comeback attempt of Nodonn. After the latter's death he became reconciled with Aiken-Lugonn and served on his High Table as Second Creator.

CENT (sahn't)   Milieu slang for the centimeter, a unit of measure. Note that cent is not used in reference to money.

CERAMETAL (ser-AM-eh-t'l)   name given to a number of extremely refractory substances, composed of ceramic permeated with carbon and metallic ions in a quasi-macromolecular structure. In the Milieu it was used for the skin of orbiter aircraft, for the "bottles" in thermonuclear reactors, for cerebroenergetic equipment, and in other applications where great resistance to heat is required. Its usual color is dull black.

CEREBROENERGETIC ENHANCER, or CE RIG a device used for greatly increasing the metapsychic output of the human brain. The golden and silver torcs technically qualify as CE enhancers, as do certain brain-boosters in common use among Milieu operants. However, the term is usually reserved for the machinery originally perfected by Marc Remillard, Jordan Kramer, and Gerrit Van Wyk, which increases the output of a single selected metafunction many hundredfold. The operator's body is placed in suspended animation through cryogenic procedures and the brain protoplasm artificially strengthened. Needle electrodes inserted into the brain "grow" an auxiliary cerebral neurostructure that transmits power to the brain from an external source. The use of a CE rig such as Marc's is extremely hazardous to all but the most powerful human operants. The device was outlawed in the Milieu after the Metapsychic Rebellion. *See also* Dermal Lavage.

CE RIG *See* Cerebroenergetic Enhancer.

CHAIM a Lowlife of Hidden Springs whose damaged eyelid was repaired by Sister Amerie.

CHALIKO (CHAL-ih-koh) name given to the genus Chalikotherium (kal-ih-koh-THEE-ree-um), which included large perissodactyls having a body that was generally horselike except for the extraordinary large claws on the three-toed feet. The domesticated chalikos ridden by the Tanu were about the size of a large draft horse, with stouter hind legs and longer forelegs than those of its equid cousin. C. goldfussi was the common Pliocene species of Europe. A related larger form, Ancylotherium, lived in eastern Europe and persisted into the Pleistocene in Africa, where it was contemporaneous with the australopithecines.

CHAN, CHEE-WU   a member of Ocala's second generation, daughter of Lu-Shen Chan and Frieda Singer-Dow. She was a self-trained scientist active in the Guderian Project.

CHAZZ   nom d'exil of a technician, a member of Basil's Bastards, killed on Monte Rosa.

CHERYL-ANN, MIZ   a lame, purblind basket maker of Hidden Springs, age 203.

CHIMAERA (ky-MEE-ruh)   a rare metapsychic phenomenon in which the physical body of the operant acquires various nonhuman characteristics—e.g., piecemeal monstrosities—as a result of subconscious creative imperatives. It is usually a symptom of profound mental dysfunction. Both Aiken Drum and the youthful Jon Remillard suffered the chimaera syndrome. The term derives from Greek myth, in which the chimaera was a female three-headed monster with body parts combining those of a lion, a goat, and a dragon. In genetics, a chimaera is an individual with mosaic characteristics.

CITY OF LIGHTS   See Finiah.

CLANA ILLUSION-SPINNER (KLAH-nuh)   a stalwart female creator and member of the Host of Nontusvel.

CLARTY JOCK   an elite gold mentioned by Vilkas.

CLAUDE   See Majewski, Claude.

CLERGY, CATHOLIC   At the time of the Saga, Catholic priests are generally called "Brother" or "Sister." The titles "Father" and "Mother" are reserved for bishops or religious superiors. The pope is "Holy Father" or "Holy Mother."

CLIFFORD   a pilot among Basil's Bastards.

COADUNATION (coh-ad-un-AY-shun)   the subtle unification process of a World or Galactic Mind. The term derives from the Latin *coadunare*, "to unite into one," and in general biology has the meaning "grown together and confluent." Coadunation implies the continuing change involved in the collective Mind's evolution. It is not in itself Unity, but leads to Unity. The proper name of the Milieu is the Coadunate Galactic Milieu. *See also* Unity.

COERCER GUILD   the second largest and most influential of the five great Guilds Mental of the Tanu. It was headed by the First Comer Leyr until he was unseated and forced into exile by the human Gomnol (q.v.). After Gomnol was killed by the Host, the presidency was decided by a duel to the death during the Last Grand Combat between the resurgent Leyr and Imidol of the Host. The latter won; but shortly afterward he was drowned in the Flood. During the reign of King Aiken-Lugonn, he himself held the office of Lord Coercer. His Second was Artigonn of Amalizan, who was killed at the Río Genil; and after him, Condateyr Fulminator of Roniah. The heraldic colors of the coercers are royal blue, or sapphire, and gold.

COERCION   one of the primary metapsychic faculties, involving the ability of one mind to influence or exert force of will upon another. The qualities called charm, charisma, animal magnetism, "presence," force of personality, and the like are all aspects of coercion, as is hypnotism. Among nonoperants, actors and great leaders are likely to have a strong coercive component to their latent armamentarium.

COLLINS, LUSK   a member of Ocala's second generation and ATV wrangler for Hagen Remillard's group of runaways. He was the son of Morrison Collins.

COMPLEXUS *See* Metapsychic Complexus.

CONCILIUM, GALACTIC the governing body of the Milieu, including magnates (members) from all racial polities. The first human magnate was Paul Remillard, father of Marc. Human magnates were greatly outnumbered by exotics in the Concilium until after the Metapsychic Rebellion.

CONDATEYR FULMINATOR (KAH'n-duh-tay'r) Tanu coercer, onetime deputy to Bormol of Roniah, who became City-Lord after Bormol drowned in the Flood. He served on Aiken's High Table as Second Coercer.

CONGREVE, COMMANDER a gold-torc human coercer operant who was garrison commandant in Goriah under Nodonn, and later held the same position under Aiken.

COSMOP WORLD Milieu slang for cosmopolitan planet, a colonial world settled by diverse ethnic groups of humanity. The cosmop worlds were apt to be those most congenial to human settlement, requiring the least amount of ecological modification. They received the first large waves of interstellar immigrants following the Great Intervention, and enjoyed the most subsidies from the exotics, since their commercial exports were most likely to be of immediate benefit to the galactic economy. The so-called ethnic worlds (q.v.) were more marginal settlement sites demanding greater stamina and resolution on the part of the pioneers.

COVENTONE PETRIFACTRIX (KOH-ven-toh'n) late mother-in-law of Parthol Swiftfoot, murdered by him on a Hunting expedition.

CRANOVEL (KRAH'n-uh-vel)   City-Lord of Darask, a PK stalwart who drowned in the Flood. He was husband to the human gold Estella-Sirone and father of Epone the Younger.

CRAZY GREGGY   *See* Greg-Donnet.

CREATIVE FLUX   the creative aspect of an individual's metafunction, especially as monitored by psychometric devices.

CREATIVITY   one of the primary metapsychic faculties, involving the ability of a mind to formulate novel ideas or exert a direct influence upon matter or energy. Creativity embraces an enormous spectrum of faculties. It ranges from artistic talent and scientific facility (both widespread among "normal" latent humans) to the awesome mindbolts of psychoenergy produced by paramount masters such as Felice and Aiken. Among the more usual operant manifestations of creativity are: shape-shifting or the generation of illusions; going invisible; producing flames, lights, or electrical bolts through simple chemical decomposition of organic or atmospheric molecules; generating a body aura; heating or cooling substances; modifying the physical appearance of substances. The less common manifestations include: interpenetration, the passing of one's body through solid matter; the genuine transmutation of matter to energy; the generation of psychocreative bubbles or other shielding; weather modification. Great talent is also required to modify organic matter that is not part of one's body. Creativity is often combined with psychokinesis in matter modification, and with redaction in the healing process.

CREATOR GUILD   the largest of the five great Guilds Mental of the Tanu. Its First Comer President was Aluteyn Craftsmaster. Later he was challenged and defeated by Mercy-Rosmar. She retained the office of Lady Creator under King Aiken-Lugonn; and after her death he himself assumed the guild presidency. Aiken's Second was the reinstated Aluteyn; and after the latter's death, Celadeyr of Afaliah. The heraldic colors of the guild were cyan and silver or white, but the membership wore a wide range of blues and greens, reflecting the individuality of their metafaculty.

CREDELA (kruh-DAY-luh)   wife to Boduragol of Afaliah, created Second Redactor by Aiken-Lugonn.

CREYN (kray'n)   a high-ranking redactor and secret member of the Peace Faction, resident in Muriah, who escorted the newly torced members of Group Green to the Tanu capital after their arrival in the Pliocene. He later became a close associate of Elizabeth. Creyn was 634 years old.

CRIARD (kree-YAH'r)   French name for a species of lutin, or hobgoblin, meaning "one who cries" or howls. *See* Howler.

CSS   in the Milieu, the designation for a commercial starship. It can be compared with PSS (polity or government starship) and XSS (private starship).

CULLUKET THE INTERROGATOR (kul-oo-KET)   Second Redactor under King Thagdal and member of his High Table, one of the principal schemers of the Host of Nontusvel. His metapsychic skills were more combatant than healing, and he was notorious for his "zealous scrutiny of pain." His torture of Felice brought about her operancy and forged a perverse bond between them. In the Postdiluvium, Culluket allied himself with Aiken and also had a peculiar affinity to Queen Mercy-Rosmar. He was the unwitting savior of Aiken's life in the fight on the Río Genil.

CUMBERLAND an "American" planet in the Human Polity, very distant from Earth.

CURTIS, DR. an ex-Rebel, once a teacher to the younger generation on Ocala, deceased by the time Group Green arrived in the Pliocene.

DACOLITE a synthetic fabric of the Milieu, usually woven to imitate tropical worsted or suitweight linen.

DAG (dah'g) the infant son of Nodonn by Huldah Henning, a tri-hybrid having Tanu, Firvulag, and human genes. He was the Battlemaster's only surviving male offspring and originally received the name Thagdal, after the late king.

DALEMBERT, BARRY a psychokinetic among Ocala's younger generation, the son of Peter Dalembert. He was the husband of Fumiko Kodama and the father of young Hope.

DALEMBERT, HOPE a member of Ocala's third generation, the three-year-old daughter of Barry Dalembert and Fumiko Kodama.

DALEMBERT, PETER PAUL ex-Rebel of Ocala, former magnate of the Concilium. He was a boyhood friend of Marc Remillard and later served the Rebellion as a psychotactician under Cordelia Warshaw. He was noted for his reckless daring, and was the primary coordinator of the escape to the Pliocene by the defeated Rebel leadership.

DALRIADA (dah'l-ree-AH-duh)   a "Scottish" planet in the Human Polity, birthplace of Aiken Drum.

DAMONE (dah-MOH'n)   redactor of Roniah, wife to the City-Lord Bormol.

DARAL (duh-RAH'l)   City-Lord of Bardelask, husband to Armida; killed in the Flood.

DARASK (duh-RAH'sk)   a small Tanu city situated on an islet at the eastern end of Lac Provençal, originally founded to safeguard traffic on the lake and the Glissade from attacks by the Famorel Firvulag. The name means "Fort Marshland." Darask stood upon the approximate site of the modern Tarascon. Its antediluvian City-Lord was Cranovel, and after the Flood it was ruled by his widow, Estella-Sirone.

DARK MOUNTAINS   a range north of the Gulf of Guadalquivir in Koneyn, a notorious haunt of "wild" Firvulag. It corresponds to the modern Sierra Morena.

DAVIES, SUE-GWEN, called **SUKEY**, dubbed **GWEN-MINIVEL** (MIH-nih-vel)   by the Tanu, a former juvenile officer on the Earth satellite colony ON-15, given a silver torc to enhance her latent redactive powers. She became the wife of Stein Oleson. After miscarrying their first son, she bore a second named Thor.

DECAMOLE (DEK-uh-moh'l)   a membranous, very thin plastic with an intricate microstructure. When inflated or pumped full of liquid it possessed remarkable rigidity and could be formed into all kinds of useful structures and appliances. These might then be collapsed after use into compact wads for extreme portability. The "skin" of decamole was virtually indestructible. It was used in the twenty-second century to make camping gear, portable shelters, boats, and the like.

DECTAR (dek-TAH'r)   female member of the Host of Nontusvel, a noted coercer and warrior.

DEDRA   See Mary-Dedra.

DEEP-REAM   See Ream.

DEINOTHERIUM (dy-noh-THEE-ree-um)   genus containing animals popularly called "hoe-tuskers," the largest elephants of the Pliocene. D. giganteum stood 5 meters or more at the withers and had great downward-curving tusks, which it might have used to dig or to break down forest growth. It was a denizen of the lowland jungles. The name is sometimes spelled dinotherium.

DEIRDRE (DEER-druh)   the Great Pyrenees sheepdog of Mercy Lamballe.

DEJAH (DEE-juh)   Sister Amerie's pet wildcat, named for Princess Dejah Thoris of E. R. Burroughs' Mars novels.

DELBAETH SHAPE OF FIRE (del-BAY'th)   a "wild" Firvulag; that is, one who rejected the sovereignty of High Vrazel. He lived among the caves of the Gibraltar Isthmus and ranged eastward through the Betics on his depredations. He was unusually strong in creativity and used psychoenergetic fireballs as weapons.

DENALI (deh-NAH-lee)   a small "American" planet of the Human Polity with a cold and rugged climate. It was the home world of Elizabeth Orme.

DEREK   nom d'exil of Derek Haas, technician, a member of Basil's Bastards.

DERMAL LAVAGE   a fluid used to preserve human epidermal tissue during the cryogenic suspension phase of cerebroenergetic enhancement. It fills both the body casing and helmet of the CE rig after the operator's circulatory system has been filled with artificial blood and the metabolic processes suspended in all except cranial tissues. The lavage soaks the pressure envelope coverall usually worn by the operator and also enters the lungs. Scanners incorporated in the coverall monitor metabolism until the refrigeration apparatus of the armor freezes solid all parts of the body except for the incandescent brain.

DESCHAMPS, GASTON (d'SHAH'm, gah-STOH'ng) —in the Milieu, director of the Immersive Pageant of Riom, France, which featured a recreation of the medieval world of A.D. 1410. Mercy Lamballe was his assistant.

DIAMOND MASK   name assumed by **Dorothea Mary Macdonald**, called **Illusio** by exotic races. She was the dirigent of Caledonia, a magnate of the Concilium and Paramount Grand Master, who became the wife of Jon Remillard and died with him in the quashing of the Metapsychic Rebellion (q.v.). In the course of saving her planet from a geophysical catastrophe early in her tenure as dirigent, she received severe injuries to the lower part of her face. She declined to have the disfigurement treated and instead wore a diamond mask. People of good will perceived through the mask illusory features of serene beauty. After her death, the exotic races proclaimed her and her husband saints and martyrs to the Unity. Her history is detailed in the second and third volumes of the Milieu Trilogy, *Diamond Mask* and *Magnificat*.

DIANE   *See* Manion, Diane.

DIARMET (d'yahr-MET) City-Lord of Geroniah, in northeast Koneyn, who survived the Flood and joined Celadeyr's traditionalist faction opposing Aiken. The return of Nodonn rekindled his hope for a return to the old ways. He participated in the aerial attack upon Aiken in Goriah and died there.

DIERDRE *See* Keogh, Dierdre.

DIGITUS IMPUDICUS vulgarly know as "the finger," an ancient gesture of insult or defiance, adopted by Aiken Drum as his heraldic cognizance when he was inducted into the battle-company of the Tanu. It remained his emblem until shortly before the Grand Tourney, when he replaced it with an open hand—the customary greeting among operant Milieu metapsychics.

DIMENSIONAL JUMPING *See* D-Jumping.

DIMORPHISM, RACIAL a significant difference of form between members of the same subspecies, two forms predominating. The Tanu and Firvulag are a dimorphic race of the species that came to be known as Homo duatensis, which also included the races of the Duat daughter-worlds. The Tanu group were typically very tall, slender, and pale-skinned, with light-colored hair and eyes, and they were metapsychically latent. The Firvulag group were of stocky build, dark-eyed in the majority, swarthy-skinned, and metapsychically operant. They varied in size: Most were of small stature (called dwarves or gnomes), others were human-sized, and some were giants (called ogres). On Duat itself, there were strict taboos against Tanu-Firvulag mating. Cross-mating did occur on the daughter-worlds, where most of the population were latents.

DIONKET (dee-on-KET) Lord Healer (President of the Redactor Guild) and First Comer, a member of Thagdal's

High Table. He was a founder of the Peace Faction but did not declare himself openly during the Times of Unrest. Together with others who had been forewarned by Brede, he survived the Flood by taking refuge in Redactor House high above the encroaching water. Later he helped guide the exodus from Aven, after which he retired to Mina-nonn's stronghold in the Pyrénées. He was frequently at Black Crag assisting Elizabeth in redactive projects, and twice helped her to save Aiken's life.

DIRIGENT (DEER-ih-jent) the primary metapsychic official of a planet in the Galactic Milieu, who provides its direct link to the Galactic Concilium. The dirigent is not a true administrator but rather a kind of overseer or ombudsman, theoretically alert to the most humble citizen's petition. The job of dirigent is one of the most taxing in human history, demanding political skill, keen insight, wisdom, and compassion. Most dirigents are women, most have creativity as their prime metafaculty, and most burn out after less than a decade in office. The most famous dirigent was Diamond Mask. The most notorious was Patricia Castellane.

D-JUMPING, also called DIMENSIONAL JUMPING hyperspatial translation by means of mind-power. The operant generates an upsilon-field by means of a rare metafaculty, passes through it into hyperspace, and by a virtuoso feat of concentration attains the objective. D-jumping was a routine accomplishment of the gigantic Ship organisms of the Duat Galaxy. Felice did it instinctively, and Marc Remillard was able to duplicate her feat by studying the mental program she used. *See also* the fourth Appendix to *The Adversary* for a more detailed discussion.

DOCILATOR a behavior-modification device that acts directly upon the brain, turning the wearer into an obedient, servile, cheerful individual with an IQ of 85 or lower. In the Milieu the docilator is used to subdue criminals or sociopaths. It can be worn temporarily or permanently implanted in the brain. Docilates are utilized as simple laborers in the Human Polity. The device was perfected by psychobiologist Sherwin H. Eisenmann, later Nobel Laureate, in the year 2068. Eisenmann's assistant, Eusebio Gomez-Nolan, later precipitated a scandal by claiming that Eisenmann had expropriated his research on the project.

DONAAR (doh-NAH'r)   a major tributary river of the Baar (Proto-Garonne), draining the Grotto Wilderness. Its name means "Cave River."

DONAL (DOH-nul)   a creator nominated City-Lord of Amalizan by Aiken.

DORSEY, properly DORSEY KODAMA   an ex-Rebel of Ocala who worked on the Mental Man project as a life-support specialist. He was the husband of Midori Kuwada and the father of Fumiko Kodama.

DOUGAL, SIR   nom d'exil of Dougal Fletcher, an eccentric medievalist and Shakespeare buff; in the Milieu a lecturer at the London School of Economics, he came to the Pliocene in search of the mystical lion Aslan. He seems to have arrived in the Many-Colored Land a few days prior to Group Green. He traveled toward Finiah with Felice and her companions, later escaping with Basil Wimborne's party. After being recaptured he was freed following Finiah's invasion and later became the companion of Tony Wayland. Eventually he attached himself to King Aiken-Lugonn as a kind of court jester.

DRAGON RANGE   a chain of low mountains along the northern side of the Aven Peninsula. Their remnants form the modern Balearic Islands.

DRUM, AIKEN, also called **AIKEN-LUGONN** (AY-kin loo-GAH'n) or **THE SHINING ONE**   a juvenile delinquent native to the planet Dalriada, condemned as a recidivist but allowed to emigrate to the Pliocene Epoch. His extraordinary latent metapsychic powers were triggered into operancy by a silver torc. His adventures are detailed in the four books of the Saga of Pliocene Exile. Another Aiken Drum is a figure in Scottish folklore, the subject of droll verses by William Nicholson in *Poetical Works* (1878). Nicholson equates Aiken Drum with the Brownie of Blednoch; a familiar Scottish nursery rhyme gives him a gentler aspect, wearing clothing composed entirely of food. The name Aiken Drum means "oak ridge" and may even have druidical connotations.

DUALITY   in metapsychology, a genuine fusion of two individual minds—such as that achieved by Felice and Culluket—not to be confused with the Unity or subsumption (qq.v.). In the Milieu, it was sometimes found among twin or other multiple-sibling operants (Dierdre and Diarmid Keogh had an imperfect duality), but rarely otherwise, and usually under pathological circumstances. The Tanu twins Fian and Kuhal were not a strict duality. Even though they were extremely interdependent, they still retained their individual personalities, one twin co-opting right-brain function and the other co-opting left.

DUAT (DOO-aht)   1. The planet of origin for the dimorphic Tanu-Firvulag race. Millions of years before Earth's time-gate to the Pliocene opened, Duat peoples colonized a widespread federation of daughter-worlds in their own galaxy. The battle-religion they espoused caused an interstellar war, after which the daughter-worlds were cut off from the home world for many generations and achieved lasting peace. When zealots from Duat attempted to reintroduce the battle-religion to the colonies, they were outlawed and pressured to give up their barbaric ways. Terms of submission included abjuration of the battle-religion and intermarriage between the Tanu and Firvulag nations, thus obliterating the basis for the original ritual conflict. The diehard remnant of Tanu and Firvulag who refused to comply was eventually transported to Earth by Brede. 2. The name Duat is also applied to the galaxy containing the Duat solar system. It is a barred spiral, smaller than our own Milky Way and some 270 million light-years distant. The Duat Confederation of six million years ago included about 11,400 inhabited worlds with a total population of 115 billion. With the Firvulag (i.e., operant) strain suppressed through intermarriage, the people were all latents who activated their metafaculties by wearing golden torcs. The blacktorc syndrome present among them serves as a genetic screening device, preventing natural operancy from remanifesting itself. This, tragically, deprives the Mind of Duat of true Unity and continuing mental evolution. Although this fact is understood by Duat savants, the people refuse to give up their torcs—this in spite of the price that must be paid by incompatible children, the ones who bear the strongest genes for operancy and resist artificial mind-amplification, with fatal consequences.

DUROFILM   a nonslick, strong plastic sheeting, used most often in the Milieu for printed matter and wrapping materials. Transparent durofilm is commonly used for windows and similar applications.

DWARF   name given to Firvulag significantly below the average human stature. Such individuals form the majority of the Firvulag nation. Cf. OGRE.

DYNAMIC FIELDS   in the New Universal Field Theory of the Milieu, are aspects of reality that form dimensional lattices that generate space, time, matter, energy, life, and mind. There are twenty-one fields designated by letters of the Greek alphabet. The first three—alpha, beta, and gamma—are "matrix" fields; the others, in various sixfold combinations, make or unmake every aspect of reality from the particle zoo to the human soul. Milieu theoreticians agree that process—continuing flux—is an essential dynamic-field characteristic, and this flow is directed toward a presumed "perfection." Most Milieu theologians place the Cosmic All/Omega/Oversoul/God within the matrix but outside the eighteen generative fields. Thus God may be said to produce the universe, yet he is not identical to it, even though it tends to evolve toward him. The elegance of the New Universal Field Theory cannot be appreciated by nonmathematical thinkers. Its full explication must be undertaken by a more skilled writer than the entertainer who produced the Saga. *See also* Lattice; Mind; Aether; Rho-Field; Sigma-Field; Tau-Field; Upsilon-Field.

DYSPROSIUM (dihs-PROH-zee-um)   a rare-earth or lanthanide element with extremely strong paramagnetic properties. Its atomic number is 66 and its atomic weight 162.51. The difficulty chemists have separating it from other rare-earth elements gave it its name, which comes from the Greek *dysprositos*, "hard to get at."

DZIEKONSKI, STAN (juh-KAH'n-skee)   one of Basil's Bastards, he captained a dreadnought-class starfighter during the Metapsychic Rebellion. He was a Milieu loyalist, as were most other inhabitants of the two "Polish" planets.

EADNAR (eed-NAH'r)   Lady of Rocilan, at the time of the Flood wife to Gradlonn City-Lord. He was drowned and Eadnar and her mother-in-law, Morna-Ia, were rescued by Alberonn. Later, he married Eadnar and they became co-rulers of the city and staunch members of Aiken's High Table. Eadnar was the sister of Tirone Heartsinger, wife to Bleyn.

EADONE SCIENCEMASTER (ee-DOH'n)   Dean of Guilds and eldest daughter of King Thagdal (by the late Queen Boanda in the Duat Galaxy). She was the highest-ranking member of Thagdal's High Table and coordinator of the activities of the five Guilds Mental. Eadone perished in the Flood.

EGG   in Milieu slang, a rhocraft flying machine, after the usual shape of the vehicle. Eggs ranged in size from personal craft about 2 meters in diameter to great egg-buses and cargo-carriers twenty times larger. All of them utilized the rho-field (q.v.) for propulsion and were "inertialess" in their operation.

EISENMANN, SHERWIN H. Milieu psychobiologist, Nobel Laureate for his perfection of the docilator (q.v.).

ELDER EARTH name given to the Milieu world six million years into the future by nostalgic Pliocene dwellers.

ELIZABETH *See* Orme, Elizabeth.

EMENDATOR a mental program to clarify farsensing— e.g., by filtering out various types of interference such as storm static, solar radiation, telepathic slopover, etc.

EMP abbreviation for electromagnetic pulse-generator, an essential component of the X-ray laser.

EMPTY SEA name given to the Pliocene Mediterranean Basin prior to the Flood. It was not completely dry, having salt lagoons in the deeper portions, fed by large continental rivers. Geologists believe that the Mediterranean dried up several times during Miocene times. This was caused by the opening and closing of the Rif and Betic Channels, which were dry land during the Pliocene. *See also* the first Appendix to *The Golden Torc*, "Apologia Pro Geologia Sua."

ENGLISH, STANDARD As a condition to acceptance in the Milieu, humanity had to become monolingual. Standard English, being the richest and most widely used tongue, was adopted universally. Other languages did not become immediately extinct, however—especially on Earth, where certain ethnic groups fiercely resisted the linguistic imposition. Nevertheless, all commerce, education, media communication, and government was swiftly converted to English. Its use was obligatory on "cosmop" planetary colonies (q.v.). Ethnic worlds were allowed a much greater leeway in retaining the old tongue as a second language. Among the greater population of the Human Polity, it became fashionable to lard one's Standard English conversation with words and phrases borrowed from other languages—especially that of one's ancestors. It was especially chic to curse in the traditional tongue, and to utilize it in making love. Nationalities particularly tenacious in adherence to their original language included the French (even those bilinguals of North America), Germans, Russians, Spanish, and Japanese. It is perhaps significant that these nations all possess a formidable quotient of ethnic dynamism.

ENGONG   an "African" planet of the Human Polity.

EPONE (eh-POH'n)   1. Coercer of Finiah, sister to Velteyn, and member of the Host of Nontusvel, killed by Felice. 2. Epone the Younger, infant daughter of Estella-Sirone and Cranovel of Darask.

ESTELLA-SIRONE (es-TEL-uh seer-OH'n)   gold-torc human operant, wife to Cranovel, City-Lord of Darask, and after his death ruler of the city. Rescued from childbed calamity by Elizabeth, she later gave Black Crag chalet to Elizabeth as a permanent retreat. Estella was a High Table member under Aiken-Lugonn.

ETHNIC WORLD   a planet of the Human Polity primarily settled by a single ethnic group, and tending to preserve certain aspects of that group's ancient cultural heritage. The criterion for an Earth nation receiving a colonial planet was "ethnic dynamism," an elusive quality that had to be certified by exotic anthropologists. A good deal of bitterness resulted when some nations were found wanting and denied a world of their own; but the Milieu's judgments were immutable, based upon adamantine logic. Nations having a high quotient of ethnic dynamism, such as the United States, Japan, Britain, and the Union of Soviet Republics, were encouraged to colonize a number of planets. The ethnic worlds were usually more difficult to settle than the cosmop worlds (q.v.). The solidarity of the colonists was deemed a boost to morale by the exotic colonial planners of the Concilium. The day-to-day operation of a typical ethnic world is detailed in the second volume of the Milieu Trilogy, *Diamond Mask*.

EVANS, GARY ex-Rebel on Ocala, originally an embryologist on the Mental Man project.

EVANS, TAFFY nom d'exil of George Gwynn Evans, former squadron leader in the Sixth Fleet of the Human Polity, who became one of Basil's Bastards.

EXALTED ONE the form of address used by bareneck or gray-torc humans to all Tanu or to silver- or gold-torc humans; and by silvers to Tanu or human golds. A Most Exalted One was a member of the High Table or a city-ruler. Because of the informality of Tanu etiquette, the form of address was often omitted or even used jocosely.

EXILE name used by time-travelers for Pliocene Earth. Even the Tanu used the term in later years.

FAFNOR ICE-JAWS (FAF-n'r) a young Firvulag hero and battle-champion, raised to this rank for prowess during the Last Grand Combat. As a novice in the Heroic Encounters, he distinguished himself by defeating Culluket.

FALEMOANA (fah-lay-moh-AH-nuh) ex-Rebel of Ocala who acted as teacher to the second generation, deceased by the time Group Green arrived in the Pliocene.

FARHAT (FAH'r-hah't) nom d'exile of a pilot among Basil's Bastards who had driven egg-buses in the Milieu.

FARSENSING a primary metafaculty embracing telepathy (farspeech), extended sight (farsight or clairvoyance), extended hearing (clairaudience), deep-sight ("X-ray" vision), and other metacommunication skills traditionally lumped under ESP, extrasensory perception. In the Milieu, such adepts are informally termed "farspeakers." The so-called search faculties also fall under farsensing and include the ability to detect an individual by means of mental signature, mass-sensing, infrared sensing, and—in the most talented—detection of minds or objects even when they are screened. Because it operates on the mental lattices of reality, farsensing is not subject to certain limitations of electromagnetic radiation and can propagate faster than light. It also propagates within hyperspace, but there is no communication possible between normal space and hyperspace. Operation of the farsenses is normally impeded by electromagnetic phenomena and by matter interposed between the farsensor and the sensed objective. It is very difficult to farsense through dense rock or metal, and cerametal (q.v.) is impervious to all but the most powerful minds. Solar radiation and storms inhibit the farsensing of mediocre minds unless an emendator program is used. A sigma-field (q.v.) shuts out all but the strongest mental probes. The farsenses have a unique brain-circuitry, peripheral to that of the other metafaculties (so-called holographic functions), and directly connected to the physical senses and the speech and image-visualization portions of the brain. Farsensing is one of the commonest human metafunctions. Even latents can "call" and be heard by an operant after suitable training.

FARSENSOR GUILD   one of the five great Guilds Mental of the Tanu. It was headed by the First Comer Mayvar Kingmaker until she was drowned in the Flood. In the Postdiluvium, Morna-Ia became President, with Sibel Longtress her Second. Because of their sensitivity and generally noncombative nature, members of this guild were prominent in the secret Peace Faction. They were not numerous in the battle-companies; but it might be noted that a female member of the Host, Riganone, was Second under Mayvar, and a noted warrior who planned to challenge her superior. The Farsensor Guild was the first to take Aiken Drum to kin, and for this reason he wore its heraldic colors, violet and gold, which he sometimes modified to black and gold.

FELDBERG in the Milieu, the highest eminence in the Black Forest at 1493 meters. During the Pliocene it is presumed to have been much higher. The Pliocene Feldberg or Meadow Mountain was the home of Sugoll and a large concentration of Howlers (q.v.). The interior of the mountain was honeycombed with caverns, both natural and artificial. Springs in the Water Caves were sources for the Ystroll and Paradise Rivers, and even for a south-flowing tributary of the Proto-Rhine.

FELICE *See* Landry, Felice.

FELIGOMPO PLANTATION (feh-lee-GAH'm-poh) a satellite of Bardelask lying on the east bank of the Rhône about 20 km north of the city. It was often used as a lunch-stop by express travelers coming down the river from Roniah.

FENNOSCANDIA during the Pliocene, the far northern portion of Europe, corresponding to the Milieu's Finland and Scandinavian nations. No Baltic Sea existed during the Pliocene, only the Anversian arm of the North Atlantic. Fennoscandia was a temperate region of lakes and low mountains having long sepulchral nights during the warm winters. The entire region was buried deep in continental glaciers during the Ice Ages. Pliocene Fennoscandia was a land of Howlers, most notably the cannibalistic Yotunag.

FERDIET THE COURTEOUS (fur-d'YET) a Tanu nominated City-Lord of Tarasiah by King Aiken-Lugonn.

FETHNEYA (feth-NAY-uh) adult daughter of Celadeyr of Afaliah and sister of Uriet. After the Flood she and

her brother were only nominally loyal to their traditionalist father.

FIAN SKYBREAKER (f'YAH'n)   identical twin brother
of Kuhal Earthshaker, son of King Thagdal and Queen
Nontusvel. A stalwart of the Host, he shared the High
Table post of Second Lord Psychokinetic with Kuhal.
Fian's left cerebral hemisphere was atrophied; his mirror-
image brother lacked a right hemisphere. Kuhal's "left
brain" function made him more adept at planning and
more verbal; Fian was more of an artistic observer and
an intuitive hedonist—hence his presence on the Delbaeth Quest. The brothers closely shared brain functions
when they were together. (*See also* Duality.) As a team,
they had a PK function second only to that of Nodonn.
Upon Fian's death, Kuhal was reduced to latency through
shock and grief. *See also* Kuhal Earthshaker.

FIELD OF GOLD   an extensive plain lying across the
River Nonol from the Firvulag city of Nionel, site of Grand
Combats in years when the Little People were frequent
victors (i.e., before the humans gave the Tanu ascend-
ancy). The Field of Gold was disused for forty years prior
to the Flood, then rehabilitated by the Howlers for the
first Grand Tourney. It received its name from the many
golden wildflowers that bloomed upon it at Combat time.

FINIAH (fih-NY-uh)   the Tanu City of Lights, the first
settlement of that nation on Pliocene Earth and their original capital city. It was the site of the only barium mine
in the Tanu kingdom, and for this reason was maintained
in illuminated splendor even when the bulk of the Tanu
population drifted toward more congenial southern lands.
Finiah became an enclave perilously surrounded by Firvulag and Howlers. Its City-Lord was Velteyn, who pre-
sided during its destruction by Lowlife and Firvulag forces.
King Thagdal intended to restore Finiah's mineworkings,
but the Flood supervened. Lowlife looting and the en-

croaching jungle reduced it to a deserted ruin. Finiah lay
on the Kaiserstuhl peninsula, near the site of modern
Freiburg.

FINNMARK a "Lapp" planet in the Human Polity.

FINODEREE (fin-NOH-dur-ee) Firvulag First Comer,
an artisan member of the Gnomish Council, husband to
Mabino. He became the foster-father of Sharn-Ador.

FIRST COMER sobriquet applied to those Tanu or Firvulag who came to Pliocene Earth on Brede's Ship. Fair
numbers of the long-lived Tanu were First Comers. There
were only a handful of distinguished First-Comer Firvulag
remaining—most notably Pallol One-Eye, Medor, Betularn of the White Hand, Mabino Dreamspinner, and Finoderee.

FIRVULAG (FEER-vuh-lah'g) or Little People, the upland racial fraction or nation of the planet Duat, who
evolved in an environment of harsh cold around the moun-
tainous polar regions of their world. The name means
"Ultimately Victorious People." Some 70 percent of the
Firvulag were shorter in stature than humanity, which
led to their being called dwarves or gnomes by the time-
travelers. About 20 percent of them had a stature close
to that of the human average; and about 10 percent were
gigantic (ogres). Their bodies were generally much more
robust than those of the Tanu and their features coarser.
Most of them had dark-brown or green eyes and brown
or reddish hair. The entire group, dwarves to giants, was
called Little People by the Tanu. (*See also* Dimorphism,
Racial.) Firvulag developed operant metafunction on Duat
as an adaptation to their terrible homeland. They were
strongest in farsensing and creativity and were fair coercers; but redaction and psychokinesis were very rare
among them. Firvulag never used torcs. Their antagonism
to the Tanu went back more than a thousand generations

on Duat, where there was never intermarriage between nations. When daughter-colonies of Duat were established on other planets, the Firvulag and Tanu strains eventually merged; but racial "purity" was maintained on the mother planet, due to the battle-religion's persistence. It must be recalled, however, that the Tanu gave birth to a Firvulag child one time in three. (Tanu mating with humans produces a Firvulag one time in seven.) Such babies were ritually turned over to the Firvulag, who accepted them fully. Brede tells the early history of the dimorphic race in *The Golden Torc*. Little People are known for their stubborn conservatism and rather crude manners. They are not as long-lived as the Tanu, nor are they as metapowerful—except for their great champions, who equal or exceed the Tanu heroes in prowess. Cannibalism was not unknown among them, although it was officially discouraged. Firvulag sexual mores were puritanically strict. The people were particularly skilled at metalcraft and jewelry making. The Firvulag capital of the Many-Colored Land was on High Vrazel Mountain (Grand Ballon, in the Vosges). Aside from this and Famorel City in the Helvetides, the Little People had very few population concentrations. Most of them lived in extended-family bands, dwelling underground in caves, burrows, or artificial mounds. Mountain Firvulag had beehive-shaped stone dwellings made without mortar. The family was the all-important social unit. Unlike the Tanu, the Firvulag had nothing resembling metapsychic guilds, nor did they have a chivalric code. Dwarves clubbed up with dwarves and ogres with ogres in the warrior battalions. Government was representative, with an elected monarchy having a sixteen-year term of office. Day-to-day affairs were handled by the Sovereign and the Gnomish Council, which included both peaceful artisans and warrior types. For the mutant Firvulag, who broke away from the main body of Little People 856 years before the action of the sage, *see* Howlers.

FITHARN PEGLEG (Fih-th'AHR'n) a one-legged Firvulag, deputized by King Yeochee IV to serve as liaison to the Lowlife humans.

FITZPATRICK, QUINN ex-Rebel at Ocala, father of Quinn Buckmaster. In the Milieu he was a talented psychobiologist, but severe brainburns suffered during the Rebellion left him enfeebled.

FLAMING MOUNTAINS the Pliocene Pyrénées.

FLASHOVER a potentially lethal disorder of metaconcert, involving the executive's loss of control over the psychoenergetic output, which thereupon "flashes" back and menaces the metaconcert members themselves.

FLECK in Milieu electronics, a microscopic component utilizing quasi-living molecules to encode data. Although expensive, they were capable of prodigious storage. For instance, Mercy Lamballe brought with her to the Pliocene a music fleck with 5Ku capacity and a library fleck holding 10Ku. Each subunit (u) represents the equivalent of ten minutes of stored audiovisual material.

FLUX-TAPPER a major component of a rhocraft propulsion system that meshes with the gravo-magnetic flux (lattices) and provides primary inertialess impetus to the vehicle. Metaphorically speaking, the flux-trapper acts like the engaging mechanism of an old-fashioned cable car, enabling the rhocraft to "attach" itself to the everflowing gravo-magnetic force-streams permeating the universe. *See also* Rhofield.

FLYING HUNT *See* Hunt.

FOG, SUMMER one of the portents of the Nightfall War in Tanu and Firvulag legend. Although a more or less permanently misty sky was typical of the Duat equatorial regions where the Tanu originated, true fog—especially during settled weather or "summer" on the exotic planet—was very rare. Pliocene Earth would have had plenty of fog during the winter rainy season; but fog during the dry summer was almost unprecedented.

FOIX (f'wah)   a "French" planet in the Human Polity.

FORESTER, SOLANGE   ex-Rebel of Ocala, late wife to Walter Saastamoinen and mother of Veikko, who took her own life in the Antarctic Isles before the coming of Group Green to the Pliocene.

FORMBY, CORNET   a silver-torc human officer killed during the siege of Finiah. Cornet was a rank roughly equivalent to lieutenant.

FORT ONION RIVER   a gray-torc outpost along the Finiah Road, lying at the western end of the Belfort Gap where the Onion River met the Lac de Bresse.

FORT RUSTY   a Lowlife settlement on the Upper Moselle, serving as a supply point and receiving depot for the Iron Villages. It was built after the fall of Finiah and abandoned shortly before the Grand Tourney after most of its inhabitants were massacred by Firvulag.

FOULETOT BLACKBREAST (FOO-lih-toh't)   Firvulag stalwart, commander of a company of Warrior Ogresses.

FOX, NANOMEA   an ex-Rebel and official of the planetary council of Okanagon, mate to Eva Smuts. Of Polynesian extraction, she was one of Kyllikki's crew.

FOX-LAROCHE, KANÉ   a young man of Ocala's second generation, the son of Nanomea Fox and Guy Laroche.

FRANCESCO, PRINCE a Lowlife killed by Howlers on the first iron-seeking expedition.

FRANCONIA a "German" planet in the Human Polity, habitat of exotic mollusks whose byssus threads provided a luxury fabric. Aiken Drum's golden suit of many pockets was made from it.

FRANCONIAN ALB in pre-Intervention days Fränkische Alb, a northeastern extension of the Swabian Alb, a low mountain range of south Germany. In the Pliocene, a haunt of Howlers.

FRITZ a guardian at Castle Gateway when Group Green arrived.

FUMIKO, properly FUMIKO KODAMA wife to Barry Dalembert and mother of Hope. A member of Ocala's second generation, she was the daughter of Dorsey Kodama and Midori Kuwada.

GALACTIC MILIEU, THE COADUNATE a benevolent federation of metapsychically operant races, dedicated to the continuing evolution of the aggregate Mind of the Milky Way Galaxy. Individual minds in the Milieu share an intimate fellowship called Unity (q.v.), which was, however, not available to the human race until after the Metapsychic Rebellion. Of the five exotic races—Lylmik, Krondaku, Gi, Poltroyans, and Simbiari (qq.v.)—all but the mysterious and ancient Lylmik have colonized hundreds of planets. Worlds unused by the exotics were carefully surveyed, especially by the methodical Krondaku, so that as other sapient races attain metapsychic operancy, they can be inducted into the Milieu and encouraged to expand their population by colonizing new planets made ready for them. Like other complex organizations, the Milieu must grow in order to survive. More than six thousand sapient races of our galaxy are being kept under surveillance by Milieu anthropologists, who patiently await psychosocial maturation. The race of one such planet, our own Earth, was adjudged by the Lylmik to possess such unusual metapsychic potential that it was invited to join the Milieu in advance of true maturation. Details of the Great Intervention are to be found in the first volume of the Milieu Trilogy, *Jack the Bodiless*. *See also* Intervention, Great. Subsequent developments in humanity's Milieu assimilation will be found in the second and third books of the trilogy, *Diamond Mask* and *Magnificat*. *See also* Rebellion, Metapsychic. The Galactic Milieu is governed by a Concilium that includes magnates—exceptional minds—of all six races. The Lylmik exert the greatest moral suasion, in spite of their relatively small numbers. They acted as the particular mentors of humanity even before the Intervention. Each planet of the Milieu enjoys considerable autonomy of government within its own racial polity (q.v.), but all are ultimately subject to the overall guidance of the Concilium and are monitored by its enforcement arm, the Magistratum. In 2110 the total population of the Milieu was about 200 billion exotics and humans. The Milieu is a structured society that certain nonmetapsychic humans have called a "benevolent despotism." It is true that lifestyles contrary to the optimal development of the Galactic Mind have been proscribed; and human reproduction is eugenically regulated. Recidivist criminals face the grim options given to Aiken Drum at the beginning of *The Many-Colored Land*. However, most human citizens, operant or not, understand the benefits of the Milieu's harmony and have no desire to oppose its ethical structure. (It should be noted that humanity's Metapsychic Rebellion took place before our operants were fully incorporated into the Unity.) While generally peaceful, the Milieu still suffers major infractions of its laws, especially among nonoperant humans and among the imperfectly operant, racially youthful Simbiari peoples. The usual penalties for minor wrongdoers are fines or public service. More serious transgressors undergo a course of re-education under skilled redactors. The Milieu's Human Polity (q.v.) is generally a free-enterprise system, although a few worlds have a cooperative economy involving specialized industries. *See also* Coadunation; Mind.

GALBOR REDCAP (GAH'l-boh'r) a Great Captain and hero of the Firvulag, a member of the Gnomish Council, husband of Habetrot.

GALEGAAR (gah-lee-GAH'r) a watercourse in Koneyn, between Tarasiah and Geroniah, having no modern analog. The name means "Hipparion River."

GALUCHOLL (GAH-loo-choh'l) a young Firvulag jeweler's assistant at the Roniah Fair.

GAMMA FOODS in the Milieu, all those sterilized by gamma radiation and packed in plastic pouches. They keep indefinitely at ordinary room temperatures. The technology for such food preservation was already available in the late twentieth century.

GARRISON, EVERETT ex-Rebel at Ocala, the mate of Ronald Inman.

GASTON *See* Deschamps, Gaston.

GATEWAY, CASTLE *See* Castle Gateway.

GATHEN, ELABY (GAH-th'n, EL-uh-bee) a member of Ocala's second generation, son of Ragnar Gathen and the mate of Cloud Remillard until he was killed at the Río Genil. Elaby was the first of the adult children to be converted by Alexis Manion away from Marc Remillard's dream of restoring Mental Man. He was a quiet young man who successfully manipulated Marc's son Hagen, although the latter was the ostensible leader of the Children of Rebellion.

GATHEN, RAGNAR ex-Rebel of Ocala and former magnate of the Concilium; he had been Chief Operations Officer of the Twelfth Fleet under Owen Blanchard. His primary metafaculties were coercion, farsensing, and PK. He never fully recovered from mental injuries suffered in the Rebellion.

GAZEBO (guh-ZEE-boh) nickname applied to the Guderian tau-field generator (q.v.) because of its superficial resemblance to an old-fashioned latticework garden structure used as a summerhouse.

GENIL, RÍO (heh-NEEL or zheh-NEEL, REE-oh) —the first pronunciation is the classic one, the second Standard English usage—a watercourse in southern Koneyn flowing northwest from Mount Mulhacén to the Gulf of Guadalquivir. Above the Pliocene Genil there took place the great fight pitting the mental forces of Aiken Drum and Marc Remillard against Felice Landry. The remains of Felice and Culluket lie alongside the river within the force-field called the room without doors.

GEORGINA team leader of a power-bore repair crew based at Lisboa, Portugal, and boss of Stein Oleson, as well as his occasional lover.

GERONIAH (jer-uh-NY-uh) a Tanu city in Koneyn situated at the eastern end of the Flaming Mountains, a center for gold mining and other mineral production. It had important lapidary workshops.

GERT (geh'rt) a Lowlife of Hidden Springs, the mate of Hansi. He participated in the sabotage attempt against the Muriah torc works.

GI (ghee) pl. & sing., a hermaphroditic exotic race of the Milieu. Its people are extremely tall and slender and have great rounded yellow eyes. Aside from their short tails and spectacular reproductive organs, the Gi are humanoid in appearance, especially when clothed. They much prefer going naked in any weather but have reluctantly bowed to human cultural mores when visiting planets of our polity. Gi are talented artists and the best farsensors in the galaxy, but they are not especially intelligent. Their temperament is emotional, supersensitive, and vacillating. Careless with the etiquette of other races, they are quick to take offense when their own customs are transgressed. The abrupt and often inconvenient onset of their mating urge is a source of vulgar humor among other races.

GIBRALTAR ISTHMUS a narrow neck of land, an extension of the Betic Cordilleran structure into the Rif Range that blocked the western end of the Mediterranean Basin during the latter Mio-Pliocene Regression. The land was then, and still is, honeycombed with caves.

GIDEON one of the original Basil's Bastards, who suffered a broken hand in a Lowlife skirmish prior to the Grand Loving and did not accompany the Second Ship's Grave Expedition.

GILLIS, SOPHRONISBA (PHRONSIE) one of Basil's Bastards, a former third engineer on a tramp starship freighter.

GLANLUIL (glah'n-l'WEEL) wife to Moreyn of Var-Mesk.

GLASS, CASTLE OF *See* Castle of Glass.

GLISSADE FORMIDABLE, LA (glee-SAH'd for-mee-DAH-b'l) name given by pioneer French time-travelers to the tremendous pouroff of the Rhône River down the European continental shelf into the nearly dry Mediterranean Basin. It means "formidable slide." In Milieu times, geologists could point out several subterranean canyons marking the changing course of the great river through the ages. It is uncertain which of these was la Glissade.

GNOME   name applied to the smaller Firvulag by time-travelers.

GNOMISH COUNCIL   the principal governing body of the Firvulag. The Little People, with their elected monarchy, were much more democratic than the Tanu. Up until the time of Sharn and Ayfa, true power resided in the Council and not in the sovereign. *See also* Yeochee IV; Sharn-Mes.

GOAL   name given by Marc Remillard to the sun of an inhabited planet, some fourteen thousand light-years from Earth, otherwise designated G3–1668 in his catalog. The Goal world was chosen by Marc to be the cradle of Mental Man after he perfected his d-jumping technique.

GODAL THE STEWARD (guh-DAH'l)   the Tanu butler at Black Crag.

GODDESS, THE   in the Tanu language **Tana**, in the Firvulag language **Té**, and in the Howler dialect **Téah**—words that all mean "goddess" or "maternal deity." The peoples of the Duat Galaxy perceived the All-in-all originally in a single aspect, that of loving sky-mother. The Goddess never became incarnate, nor did she have a complex theology or a priestly hierarchy. Nevertheless her changing modes of worship had a profound influence upon the two Duat nations. In the most primitive times, before the colonization of the daughter-worlds, the Goddess was one. Later, when racial dimorphism arose, the planet harbored antagonistic Tanu ("Children of the Goddess") and Firvulag ("Ultimately Victorious People") strains, and the aspect of the Goddess was seen as catastrophically cleft in twain (Tana and Té, Sisters in Shadow). Mundane hostility between the upland and lowland subraces developed into a genuine battle-religion (q.v.). It was believed that the conflict would eventually culminate in the Nightfall War, which would reunite the double Goddess into one and engender a new and perfected Duat people. The battle-religion was exported to the daughter-world colonies and led to an interstellar war that the colonies perceived as Nightfall. The planet Duat was isolated, but the old battle-religion persisted among Tanu and Firvulag. After many generations, when the daughter-worlds underwent a spiritual reformation as well as a technoeconomic rebirth, the people of the colonies were again monotheistic; racial dimorphism had vanished in a great melting pot and the Goddess was one. She was worshipped as a cosmological principal under three aspects: Mother of All, Mover of All, and End (Product, Consumer, Engulfer) of All. She was eventually seen as an Absolute from which all reality came and to which it tended. Her trinity was amplified thus: 1. As Creator or Feminine Principle she gave life, sustained it, embraced it unendingly; her symbol is Ocean. 2. As Mover or Masculine Principle, she was First Cause, instigator, font of authority, source of wisdom; her symbol is Wind. 3. As Divine Child (begotten by herself) she was fruit of love, savior, bridge, channel of grace; her symbol is Rainbow, which is a transfiguration of water and air (her first and second aspects) by light—which equates with dynamic love. *See also* Battle-Religion; Nightfall War; Peace Faction.

GODDESS MOUNTAINS   name given by the Firvulag to the Helvetides or Pliocene Alps.

GOMEZ-NOLAN, EUSEBIO   *See* Gomnol.

GOMNOL, properly SEBI-GOMNOL (SAY-bee GOMnoh'l) Lord Coercer, Tanu sobriquet adopted by **Dr. Eusebio Gomez-Nolan**, who became the powerfully operant human President of the Coercer Guild. In the Milieu

he was a psychobiologist and a co-developer of the docilator (q.v.). Bitter when his superior, Eisenmann, was
honored and his own role slighted, he came to the Pliocene
about forty years prior to the arrival of Group Green.
Fascinated by the psychoamplifying torcs, he plunged into
intensive research, which the Tanu encouraged. His first
triumph was a signal improvement in the rama torcs, which
resulted in his being awarded a golden torc, at the time
a very rare honor among time-travelers. Gomnol was the
first human with strong latencies to be lifted to operancy
by the torc. His extraordinary powers shocked the Tanu
and made the prudent among them (notably Nodonn) very
uneasy. Continuing his researches, Gomnol developed both
the gray torcs and the silver torcs with their mind-con-
trolling circuitry. He also invented a mental assay device
used for the classification of arriving time-travelers.
Eventually he became Second Lord Coercer under Leyr,
a position he held at the advent of Marc Remillard and
the defeated Metapsychic Rebels. Leyr was seriously injured in a skirmish with the human operants. Gomnol
seized the opportunity to advance his own position, and
the following year defeated Leyr in the Manifestation of
Power, becoming Lord Coercer. Gomnol's later history
is detailed in *The Golden Torc*.

**GORCHAKOV, BROTHER ANATOLY SEVERINOV-
ICH, O. F. M.** (GOH'r-chuh-kof, ah-nuh-TOH-lee sev-
rin-OH-vich) a priest of the Observant Friars Minor
(Franciscans) who in the Milieu was a bureaucrat in the
Siberian Roman Catholic Primacy, Yakutsk. He was an
early time-traveler, having perceived a vocation to make
the Pliocene his parish ministry. He was based in Finiah,
and with the assent of the Tanu became a circuit rider
throughout the northerly regions of the Many-Colored
Land. He met Sister Amerie after the Flood when she
stopped at the Castle Gateway refugee center. Amerie
convinced the tough old man to attempt Elizabeth's spiritual reclamation.

GORDON   a silver-torc redactor at Redactor House in Muriah.

GORF   a jocose Milieu slang name for a citizen of French extraction, derived from the reversed spelling of an ancient pejorative. The term was used by North American hockey fans as early as 1960.

GORIAH (goh-RY-uh)   the second largest Tanu city, seat of Nodonn Battlemaster. Its name means "Sea City." After the Flood it was taken over by Aiken-Lugonn and made capital of his kingdom. Goriah lay on a promontory overlooking the Strait of Redon in western Armorica. It was surrounded by rich mines and plantations. Inland from it, near the banks of the Laar River, was the Grove of May, a Goriah trust. Goriah was supplied by sea and by barges on the Laar. Its citadel, the Castle of Glass, was perhaps the most splendid edifice in the Many-Colored Land.

GRADLONN (grah'd-LAH'n)   City-Lord of Rocilan and husband of Eadnar, he was the son of Morna-Ia. Gradlonn drowned in the Flood.

GRAND COMBAT   the annual ritual war of the battle-religion (q.v.) and most sacred season of the Many-Colored Land. It took place in mid autumn over a five-day period. The first day—usually 31 October or 1 November in the synchronous Milieu—began at dawn on the day that the Mouthpiece Star of the Trumpet (hiding the distant Duat Galaxy) had its midnight culmination above the High Vrazel–Finiah meridian. The Combat was preceded and followed by a one-month Truce to accommodate travel to and from the designated battlefield. Traditionally, the war was fought upon the field of the nation that had been victorious in the last year's contest. The Tanu owned the White Silver Plain near Muriah and the Firvulag owned the Field of Gold near Nionel. Beginning with the Opening of the Sky, the Combat's First Day included nonlethal sporting events. The Second Day, in pre-time-gate years, was a showcase of novice warriors called the Low Mêlée, featuring battles to the death between small groups or pairs of antagonists. After humanity arrived, the Low Mêlée featured only gray-torcs and was called the Contest of Humans. The latter part of the Second Day saw the choice of Combat leaders by both Tanu and Firvulag. Practically, these Great Captains had been chosen long years before and only stood forth to dare any challenge to their authority. If there was a challenge, both claimants demonstrated mental prowess in the Manifestation of Power. Optionally, the rivals could duel to the death during the Combat itself. The Second Night featured a War Feast for each nation and invocations to the Goddess of Battles. The Third Day initiated the Combat proper or High Mêlée, in which Tanu and Firvulag went at each other physically and mentally with the object of decapitating the Foe. Heads were tallied and cataloged according to rank—the least points for a gnomish warrior or knight bachelor and the most for a hero of the High Table or Gnomish Council. (This cult of the severed head can be compared to a similar battle practice observed by Julius Caesar among the Celts.) The Combat was recessed at sunrise and sunset of the Fourth and Fifth Days to allow succor of the wounded and gathering of the corpses to fuel the eventual bonfire beneath the Great Retort. The Mêlée featured only gray-torcs and was called the Contest hours until dawn were devoted to the Heroic Encounters, duels between Tanu and Firvulag battle-champions that were usually decided on points. These were ordinarily nine encounters, but the Last Grand Combat featured only eight because of the rivalry between Tanu battle-master aspirants, which occasioned the "bumping" of the most junior Firvulag hero. The winner of the Encounter of Battlemasters presented his sovereign with the loser's banner. The custodian of the Sword (Eadone among the Tanu, Betularn among the Firvulag) presented this Grand Combat trophy to the victorious battlemaster, who would pass it in a gesture of fealty to his king. As the pyre beneath the Retort was ignited, the Combat would end with the singing of the Song. In the rare case when a battlemaster of the Tanu aspired to the kingship himself, he would do as Aiken Drum did at the climax of *The Golden Torc*. The ruler of the Combat-victorious nation might style himself High King throughout the following year.

GRAND LOVING, also called GRAND LOVE FEAST the second great ritual season of the Tanu and Firvulag, which the nations celebrated separately. It took place when the Mouthpiece Star made its noon culmination above the High Vrazel–Finiah meridian—usually 30 April or 1 May in the synchronous Galactic Milieu. The Tanu gathered at the Grove of May near Goriah and the Firvulag at High Vrazel or Nionel. The Loving was a time for marriages and jollification—sedate and family-style among the Firvulag and wildly erotic among the Tanu. Firvulag were strict about having the betrothed wait until the Loving for their nuptials. Tanu might marry at other times of the year, but the union was solemnized at the Loving. The Tanu Maypole and the Firvulag twin fires of fertility persisted in human folklore into the twentieth century. No Truce accompanied the antediluvian Loving; but the Hunt was forbidden during the three days of celebration.

GRAND MASTER in the Milieu, a title given to the second highest rank of metapsychic practitioners, those who were honored as standing at the peak of their profession. Raw power alone did not merit grandmastership. There was a long novitiate before a candidate attained Adept status, after which one might aspire to Master and Grand Master. The highest category was the Grand Master Magnates, who served on the Concilium (q.v.). Leaders among these were historically designated Paramount

Grand Master; but after the Rebellion, the title was only given honoris causa and did not indicate superior rank.

GRAND TOURNEY   King Aiken-Lugonn's novel celebration, instituted after the Flood as a peaceful substitute for the Grand Combat. It was to be an occasion of heartfelt rivalry between Tanu and Firvulag, but (largely) nonlethal. Victory would be awarded on point scoring, and the trophy was to be the Singing Stone. Although the Tourney was considered blasphemous and heretical by diehard traditionalists, there was precedent for this sublimation of the battle-religion in certain festivals held on the daughter-worlds of Duat. The idea for a Grand Tourney was originally proposed in the Many-Colored Land by Minanonn the Heretic during the Times of Unrest. Peace Faction members suggested it to Aiken; the Firvulag assent was typically perfidious, since they planned to use it as a pretext for Nightfall.

GRAVOMAG REPULSOR   a type of force-field used for pushing or fending off matter. It combines aspects of the sigma-field with certain zeta and lambda components of the lattice meshings.

GRAY LIMBO   *See* Hyperspace.

GREAT BRACKISH MARSH   before the Flood, a region in the western Mediterranean Basin, south of the Betic Cordillera, where the Proto-Andarax River poured into a salty lagoon. It was less inimical to life than other parts of the Empty Sea and supported a varied flora and fauna.

GREAT INTERVENTION   *See* Intervention, Great.

GREAT LAGOON   before the opening of Gibraltar, that part of the Mediterranean Basin west of the Isle of Kersic, containing residual bodies of intensely salty water. The Great Lagoon during the Pliocene was far below sea level, but its floor was not then so deep as it is now. Except near the outflow of continental rivers, the waters of the Lagoon approached a salinity of 27 percent and were continually precipitating. Only a handful of saline-tolerant organisms lived at the Lagoon margins. The shallowest parts had a milky look, but the depths were pale blue. Around the Great Lagoon were to be found salt flats, gypsum and salt dunes, and grotesquely formed evaporite structures having pale, colored strata.

GREAT ONE a term used, especially among the Firvulag, for persons of nobility. It was also sometimes used by humans as a synonym for Exalted One (q.v.).

GREAT ORDEAL a rare religious event among the Tanu and Firvulag, a ritual duel of battlemasters in which the survivor voluntarily lays down his life, accepting a blast from his own photon weapon. The defunct hero is seen as a messenger to the Goddess, usually commemorating some pivotal event in race history. A Great Ordeal upon Pliocene Earth followed the establishment of the first Tanu and Firvulag settlements. It took place at the Ship's Grave and was fought by Sharn the Atrocious and Bright Lugonn. Lugonn, the victor, was declared to be the Ship's captain through eternity, a thank-offering for the successful colonization of the Many-Colored Land and for the Ship who carried the people to their exile.

GREATOREX, ALICE A chemical engineer at the Fennoscandia mine.

GREAT RETORT a large glass structure, resembling a box, in which prisoners were confined during the Grand Combat. It stood upon a scaffold, and bodies of the slain were heaped under it and torched at the Combat's close. Among those condemned to the Retort were criminals, traitors, cowards, and the mentally ruined. Deposed royalty or guild presidents might optionally choose immolation as an alternative to banishment.

GREAT SOUTH ROAD   a principal thoroughfare of the Many-Colored Land, beginning at Roniah and extending along the west bank of the Rhône to Sayzorask at Lac Provençal. Below Sayzorask the road trended west, meandering down to its terminus at Afaliah. The South Road was a wide graded track, nowhere paved, secured by small forts in the wilder regions. Other roads connecting to it were the Aven Road along the Balearic Peninsula; the Northern Track to Finiah; and the Western Track to Burask and the head of navigation on the Laar River. A short spur led to Amalizan and Sasaran.

GREAT WATERFALL   a stupendous cascade created by the sundering of the Gibraltar Isthmus, admitting Atlantic waters to the nearly dry Pliocene Mediterranean Basin. When Hagen Remillard viewed it, it was 9.7 km wide by 822 meters high. The Great Waterfall may have endured for less than 100 years before filling the New Sea. A sill still exists between the Pillars of Hercules, which inhibits the flow of oceanic waters into the Mediterranean, even though the basin itself has subsided considerably since Pliocene times.

GREG-DONNET (greh'g DAH-net) **GENETICS MASTER,** Tanu sobriquet adopted by GREGORY PRENTICE BROWN, M.D., PH.D., D.SC., L.H.D., once Professor of Human Genetics at Johns Hopkins University and a skillful analyst of genetic evolutionary trends. He was among the earliest human immigrants to the Pliocene and became intrigued by the reproductive problems of the Tanu and the unexpected compatibility of exotic germ plasm with our own. Because of his valuable researches into Tanu-human hybridization, he was granted a golden torc, the first human so honored. He possessed no significant metapsychic latencies, and the torc had the unfortunate effect of exacerbating his already eccentric personality. In spite of frequent fits of zaniness, he was able to continue his work. He was held in fond esteem by the Tanu royalty, who called him Crazy Greggy. A member of the Creator Guild, he was a fascinated observer of the rise of Tanu hybrids to eminence in the Many-Colored Land. Katlinel the Dark-eyed was his special protegée, and he accompanied her when she eloped with the Howler prince, Sugoll. Greg-Donnet was touched by the mutants' predicament. In Nionel he developed a successful Skin-tank for modifying Howler deformities and also encouraged the mating of humans and Howlers.

GRENFELL, BRYAN   a doctor of cultural anthropology who specialized in culture-conflict studies; he was one of the members of Group Green. His history is detailed in *The Many-Colored Land* and *The Golden Torc*.

GRESSON (greh-SOH'n)   name given to a river and to the Monte Rosa glacial icefall that is its source. The Gresson corresponds to the modern Lys River in northern Italy.

GRINTLASKIN (grint-LAH-skin)   the uniquely "breathable" but waterproof hide of the grintla, an animal native to the cosmop planet Elysia. Rainwear made of this material is valued throughout the Human Polity.

GROTTO WILDERNESS   a dense jungle north of the River Donaar in France. In the synchronous Milieu year 2083 it was the scene of a battle between survivors of the Metapsychic Rebellion under Marc Remillard and Tanu forces led by Nodonn.

GROUP GREEN   arbitrary designation given to the eight persons passing through the time-gate on 25 August 2110. It included: Aiken Drum, Bryan Grenfell, Felice Landry,

Claude Majewski, Stein Oleson, Elizabeth Orme, Annamaria Roccaro, and Richard Voorhees. It was customary for a single group to pass through the gate at dawn on each day of the week. Madame Guderian used spectrum colors to code the week's bag: violet, indigo, blue, green, yellow, orange, red.

GROVE OF MAY   an area in the forest along the Lower Laar River, some 40 km east of Goriah, site of the annual Tanu Grand Loving.

GUADALQUIVIR, GULF OF (g'wah-thal-kih-VEER) during the Pliocene, a great arm of the Atlantic Ocean extending some 250 km into western Koneyn, analogous to the modern valley of the Río Guadalquivir. During the geological epoch immediately preceding the Pliocene, the waterway was open all the way to the Mediterranean.

GUDERIAN, ANGÉLIQUE MONTMAGNY, called "MADAME" (goo'd-ree-ANg or goo-DARE-yun)   —the first her pronunciation, the second the Standard English rendition—wife to Professor Théophile Guderian, and a colleague with him at the Institute for Dynamic-Field Studies in Lyon, France. After his death she appropriated his time-gate apparatus and established l'Auberge du Portail, which she operated for nearly sixty-five years, sending almost one hundred thousand time-travelers to the Pliocene Exile. In 2106, when she was 127 years old (twice rejuvenated), she herself passed into the Pliocene. Her history is detailed in *The Many-Colored Land* and *The Golden Torc*.

GUDERIAN TAU-FIELD GENERATOR   the proper name of the machine that formed the time-gate, a one-way passage from the France of the Galactic Milieu to the Pliocene Epoch six million years earlier. In principle, Guderian's device was similar to a hyperspatial translator, except that its superfices led into a hypertemporal matrix (gray limbo) rather than a hyperspatial matrix. Alex Manion's genius helped the young adults of Ocala's second generation to modify Guderian's design so the machine would send travelers into the future. *See also* Tau-Field.

GUDERIAN, THÉOPHILE inventor of the tau-field generator, he was a professor and director of the Institute for Dynamic-Field Studies at the University of Lyon at the time of the Intervention. In the subsequent years of the "knowledge explosion" he perfected his device, which was first demonstrated in 2034. His colleague and wife was Angélique Guderian. After his health failed he retired to a country home in the Monts des Lyonnais. Because the time-travel machine seemed to have no practical application, he was allowed to take it with him for additional research, retaining an emeritus position at the Institute. Later, the equipment was deeded to him outright in recognition of his achievement. He died in 2041.

GUERCIO (g'WEH'r-chee-oh) nom d'exil of a vendor of ice confections in Goriah. The nickname means "cross-eyed."

GUILDS MENTAL the five great metapsychic fellowships of the Tanu, having a clan structure. They included the Guilds of the Coercers, Creators, Farsensors, Psychokinetics, and Redactors. Guild members often felt a greater affinity for each other than for their natural relatives. In social situations, it was common for all Tanu to refer to one another by guild designation—e.g., Creative Sister or Redactive Brother. The guilds were under the overall supervision of Eadone Sciencemaster. *See also* Coercer Guild; Creator Guild; Farsensor Guild; Psychokinetic Guild; Redactor Guild.

GULDENZOPF, UWE (GUH'l-d'n-tsoh'pf, OO-vuh) a Lowlife of Hidden Springs, head of Hunting and Public Safety on the village Steering Committee and a fighter under Chief Burke, known for his habit of smoking a meerschaum pipe. He was part of the force that invaded the Muriah torc works.

GYRE OF COMMERCE   a ring-shaped street surrounding an open plaza in the heart of Goriah, the principal business district and social center of the Tanu city. All roads leading into Goriah terminated at the Gyre.

HABETROT (HAH-bee-trah't)   wife to the Firvulag ogre Galbor Redcap.

HAKKINEN, RAIMO (HAH-kee-nen, RAY-moh)   a Finno-Canadian forester of British Columbia, torced with silver in virtue of his weak PK faculty. He became a crony of Aiken Drum. During the Last Grand Combat he was caught malingering and condemned to the Retort. Saved by the Flood, he joined Aluteyn's band and helped conquer Calamosk. His insolence later caused his banishment from the city and he came to Goriah and joined Aiken's Elite Golds as an officer.

HAMID   a Lowlife at Iron Maiden village in charge of the turpentine still.

HANSI (HAH'n-see)   Lowlife of Hidden Springs, mate of Gert, who was a member of the force invading the Muriah torc works.

HARRY   a Cockney boatman on the River Rhône, who succumbed following mental abuse by Felice.

HAUT FOURNEAUVILLE (OH fur-no-VEEL)   or "Blast-Furnace Town," one of the Iron Villages of the Moselle River.

HEAD   Milieu slang for an individual strong in a particular metafaculty; e.g., a PK-head is a powerful psychokinetic.

HELLADOTHERIUM (HEH-lah-doh-THEE-ree-um) or **HELLAD**   a genus of large giraffids with short necks. H. duvernoyi, the common Pliocene species, is present in Greek fossil beds. The domesticated hellads of the Many-Colored Land had the proportions of the modern okapi but were the size of robust camels. The Tanu used them for draft animals or beasts of burden. Because of their jouncing gait they were not ridden.

HELVETIDES (hel-VEH-tih-deez)   name given to the Swiss Alps during the Pliocene. One school of geologists would reserve the term for the northernmost nappes of the western Alps, with the southerly nappes (including Monte Rosa) designated Pennides. Time-travelers were more cavalier and called the entire region between the Jura and the Po Basin Helvetides.

HEMATITE (HEE-muh-ty't)   one of the Iron Villages of the Moselle River.

HENNING, HULDAH   a hybrid woman who cared for Nodonn during his convalescence on Kersic. She conceived his child. Huldah was the daughter and granddaughter of Isak Henning. Her grandmother was a hybrid Firvulag, child of a Tanu father and human mother. Huldah was of gigantic stature, showing mostly Firvulag traits.

HENNING, ISAK   an elderly human, father and grand-father of Huldah, who fled to Kersic after a sojourn as a bareneck antelope herder on Aven.

HERCULES CLUSTER   a globular star cluster in the constellation Hercules, also called M13 or NGC6205. It is some twenty thousand light-years from our solar system. In 1974 the great radio telescope at Arecibo, Puerto Rico, directed a message at this cluster. In the Milieu, there were a handful of human colonies there.

HERCYNIAN FOREST (hur-SEE-nee-un)   name given by the time-travelers to the subtropical forest in the region between the Vosges and Armorica, below the Paris Basin.

HERENDORF (HAIR-un-dorf)   a powerful painkilling medication of the Milieu pharmacopoeia.

HEROIC ENCOUNTERS   the finale of the Grand Combat, pitting Tanu heroes against Firvulag in single combat and winding up with the Encounter of Battlemasters. The contests were scored high and usually decided on points.

HEYMDOL BUCCINATOR (HAY'm-dul BOO'k-sin-ay-t'r)   Tanu Marshal of Sport, nominated City-Lord of Geroniah by Aiken-Lugonn.

HIBERNIA   an "Irish" planet of the Human Polity.

HIDDEN SPRINGS   the principal Lowlife settlement, which became the Pliocene home of Madame Guderian, Chief Burke, Sister Amerie, and many other characters of the Saga. It was situated deep in the Vosges Mountains and lay approximately on the site of the charming Milieu spa, Plombières-les-Bains. It had many hot and cold springs.

HIGHJOHN, SKIPPER   boatman on the Rhône who conveyed Creyn's party to Muriah.

HIGH KING in strict exotic practice, the monarch of the nation victorious in that year's Grand Combat.

HIGH MÊLÉE in the Grand Combat, the principal phase of fighting between Tanu and Firvulag battle-companies, scored by the taking of heads.

HIGH TABLE among the Tanu, a body including the highest-ranking nobility, who sit with the king at official functions and have a certain administrative role under his sovereignty. Unlike the Gnomish Council of the Firvulag, the High Table was not a genuine governing body. It could recommend action but the final disposition rested with the king. Practically, the presidents of the five great Guilds Mental were autonomous in guild affairs, so long as these did not conflict with royal policy. Under Thagdal, the High Table included twenty seats: guild presidents and their seconds, and certain fighting specialists. Under Aiken-Lugonn, the City-Lords were elevated and the fighters eliminated. High Table members were addressed as Most Exalted.

HIGH VRAZEL (VRAY-zul) the first Firvulag settlement on Pliocene Earth and capital of the nation, situated on Grand Ballon mountain in the Vosges. The proper name in Firvulag is Hy-Vrazel (hee-VRAY-zul), meaning "Lofty Citadel." But the Lowlives' Standard English corruption is used throughout the Saga. Many of the city's dwellings were hollowed out of solid rock. The royal palace itself lay deep within the mountain, which retained an eldritch reputation even into Milieu times.

HIPPARION (hih-PAY-ree-un or hih-PAH-ree-un) the first pronunciation proper for the genus, the second usual among Pliocene humans—the pony-sized, three-toed horse widespread during the Miocene and Pliocene. The typical species of Europe was H. gracile, which lived in vast herds that left extensive fossil remains and gave its name to the famous "Hipparion Fauna" of the epoch. The little horses were an important source of meat for the exotic races. They were not domesticated by the Tanu because of their small size, but later, the dwarf Firvulag began taming them.

HLITHSKJALF MASSIF (h'LITH-sk'yah'lf) *See* Asgard.

HOBBINO (hah-BEE-noh) Firvulag of Monte Rosa, wife to Purtsinigelee.

HOE-TUSKER *See* Deinotherium.

HOFGARN (HAW'f-gah'rn) dwarf servitor to King Sharn and Queen Ayfa.

HOMI a Lowlife ironworker, of Sri Lanka in the Milieu, who distinguished himself during the Finiah invasion.

HOOBY (HOO-bee) exotic name for the fungus Amanita muscaria, the fly amanita, widespread in Europe and Asia even into Milieu times. It has a scarlet or orange cap flecked with white. Although poisonous to humans except when ingested in the most minute quantities, the mushroom was esteemed by the Firvulag and some Tanu for its intoxicating and psychedelic qualities. On Elder Earth, the mushroom was early used in magical rites; it may be the Indian "soma." East European peoples associated it with Winter Solstice rituals, and it was later a common subject for Christmas Tree ornaments! It is interesting to note the persistence in Slavonic languages of the word hooby; e.g., the Polish hubka, Czech houba, Bohemian houby, etc.

HORVATH, IMRE a member of Ocala's second generation, the son of John Horvath.

HORVATH, JOHN   ex-Rebel of Ocala, former officer in the Rebel armada.

HOST OF NONTUSVEL   the 242 adult children of Queen Nontusvel and King Thagdal who formed a power-faction that schemed to establish a dynasty in contravention of Tanu custom. Nontusvel's was a record progeny among royal spouses, and it was falsely claimed that none of her brood was a psychic weakling. Oldest and leader of the Host was Nodonn Battlemaster. Other stalwarts included Culluket, Imidol, Kuhal and Fian, Epone, Velteyn of Finiah, and Riganone. Except for Kuhal and Culluket, all but fifteen members of the Host perished in the Flood.

HOUGHMAGANDY (HO'kh-muh-GAH'n-DEE)   Scottish term for sexual adventuring.

HOWLER or HOWLING ONE   one of the mutant race of Firvulag who broke away from the main body of the nation some 140 years after the first arrival of the exotics upon Pliocene Earth. They opposed the Grand Combat and were the Firvulag equivalent of the Tanu Peace Faction. Unfortunately, the core group chose to settle around the Feldberg, where radioactive mineral deposits caused deleterious mutations in the sensitive exotic germ plasm. Most of the Howlers became monsters of widely varying aspect. They spread out from the Feldberg into many parts of Europe, but were especially abundant in the northeastern regions. Most were solitary or lived in small family bands. The exception was the concentrated population in and about the Feldberg (Meadow Mountain) itself. In spite of their physical repulsiveness, Howlers loved gorgeous dress and jewelry. They were expert miners and costume makers and decked themselves out splendidly. The material prosperity of Sugoll and his people exceeded that of the Firvulag court, since Howlers did not incur the annual expense of the Grand Combat. The mutants received their common name from their habit of uttering eerie lamentations, a kind of racial dirge. The Yotunag, great monsters of the northlands, were cannibals; but most other Howlers were reasonably peaceable unless provoked by Tanu or by their Firvulag kin. They were nominally included under the sovereignty of High Vrazel but actually took no part in Firvulag affairs until after the Flood. Madame Guderian called them les Criards, a name given to malevolent goblins in French folklore. Other Milieu nations also had traditions of them. *See also* Sugoll; Greg-Donnet.

HUAL GREATHEART (h'WAH'l)   a senior member of the Host, deputy to Nodonn in Goriah at the time Marc Remillard and his defeated Rebels arrived in the Pliocene. He was killed in a skirmish with the operant humans.

HUB   the central region of the Milky Way Galaxy, in which a few precarious human colonies were established and later abandoned. Cosmic radiation among the densely packed stars of the Hub inhibited human reproduction, although it was not apparently harmful to the exotic coadunate races. Human genetic fragility seems to be a Tanu heritage.

HUBERT   a crust driller of Lisboa Metro in the Milieu, an associate of Stein Oleson.

HULDAH   *See* Henning, Huldah.

HUMAN POLITY   a confederation, or racial community, of the Galactic Milieu, including the 783 planets colonized by humanity since the Intervention, plus Earth. The operation and early history of the Human Polity are detailed in the Milieu Trilogy. *See also* Galactic Milieu; Polity.

HUNT   the ritual sport of the Tanu, involving the tracking and decapitation of Firvulag, Howlers, Lowlife humans, or formidable wild animals—in descending order of prey value. Originally, the Hunt took place afoot and Firvulag ogres were active predators. Later, when the Tanu were mounted upon chalikos, they had a tremendous sporting advantage over the Little People. The greatest Tanu heroes, such as Nodonn, Velteyn, and the twins Kuhal and Fian, had Flying Hunts, airborne by psychokinesis. A Grand Hunt, or Quest, was a particularly elaborate expedition, such as a punitive foray against some Firvulag faction or individual. Hunts could take place at any time except during Grand Combat or its flanking Truces, or during the three days of the Grand Loving. One could compare the Hunt with the "faery rade" of Celtic folklore, and with das Wütende Heer of German tales, and the Accursed Huntsman of the French. King Aiken-Lugonn abolished the Hunting of rational beings.

HURLEY, HURLING, or SHINTY a no-holds-barred form of football anciently popular among the Tanu and Firvulag. It originally used a freshly severed giant head (which deteriorated to a skull) instead of a ball. A similar game, called hurley among the Irish or shinty among the Scots, used a bat shaped like a hockey stick for belaboring the ball. Gaelic-rules football is much closer to the original exotic game, which always featured riotous action and mayhem among players and bystanders. Celtic faery folk were great hurlers and sometimes included humans in the game. The slang terms hurley-burley, hullabaloo, shinny, and shindig all derive from this rugged sport.

HUSQVARNA, HUSKY (HUSS-k'vah'r-nuh) *See* Stun-Gun.

HYAINAILOUROS (hy-AY-nay-LOO-roh's) genus containing an enormous saber-toothed mammal of the Upper Miocene of Africa and Asia, placed among the felids by Romer. It seemed to combine hyaenid and catlike aspects.

HYBRID   in the Many-Colored Land, a term used for persons of mixed Tanu and human heritage. At first only human males engendered hybrid offspring. Later, when the sterility of female time-travelers was reversed by the physician Anastasya Astaurova, human women were used in Tanu breeding schemes; they were much more fertile than Tanu women. The hybrids tended to be more robust physically than the purebloods. They also had more abundant body hair and sometimes dark-colored eyes. Hybrid children were almost never subject to the black-torc syndrome that afflicted purebloods. Hybrids tended to exceed in the coercive and creative metafunctions. Three metapowerful hybrids—Bleyn, Alberonn, and Katlinel— were members of King Thagdal's High Table. Initially, there was social prejudice against hybrids. This was officially forbidden by King Thagdal, but nevertheless persisted. The most spectacular hybrids were those of Tanu and black-human extraction, such as Alberonn Mindeater, who had chocolate skin in combination with the pale Tanu hair and eyes. Since Tanu-human matings might produce a Firvulag recessive, there were hybrids among the Firvulag, too; but the wide variation in body type among the Little People made such persons virtually unnoticeable among purebloods of the nation. Hybrids were less sensitive to iron poisoning than purebloods, and less sensitive to water immersion. A disproportionate number of hybrids survived the Flood for this reason.

HYENA   the most common carnivore of the Pliocene, with many species common and widespread. The dwarf hyena of North Africa encountered by Hagen's caravan was Ictitherium. The huge Percrocuta eximia was a noteworthy European species, with a mandible 23 cm long and a massive, short-backed body.

HYPERSPACE, or HYPERSPATIAL MATRIX   also called subspace, the "hype," the matrix, or the gray limbo, a quasi-dimensional medium nodally integrated with "normal" space, and, like it, generated by spatio-temporal dynamic-field lattices. Hyperspace has its own time-frame and space-frame and may be thought of as lying "outside" of normal space-time. The hyperspatial matrix is a mathematical concept belonging to the New Universal Field Theory. It was routinely utilized in the Milieu by superluminal starships, which entered into it by means of an upsilon-field (q.v.) gateway. For a general description of hyperspatial translation, see the fourth Appendix to *The Adversary*. *See also* D-Jumping; Dynamic Fields; Lattice.

HYPERSPATIAL TRANSLATION   *See* forth Appendix to *The Adversary*.

IBERIA RIVER *See* Ybaar.

IDFS initials of Institute for Dynamic-Field Studies, a Milieu organization harboring large numbers of Rebels prior to 2083.

ILLUSIO, SAINT name given to Diamond Mask by exotic peoples of the Milieu after her death in the Rebellion. *See* Diamond Mask.

ILMARY (eel-MAH-ree) Howler miner at the Fennoscandian dysprosium diggings.

IMIDOL (IH'm-ee-daw'l) youngest member of the Host of Nontusvel, Second Coercer under Gomnol, who briefly became Lord Coercer by defeating his rival Leyr in the Last Grand Combat.

IMMERSIVE PAGEANTS in the Milieu, a series of ethnic "theme parks," usually scattered about the appropriate nations of Old Earth, featuring re-creations of the ancient national heritage. The pageants cater to tourists from the colonial planets and to visiting exotics. Mercy Lamballe was an associate director of one of the French pageants. Visitors to the pageant might simply observe the activities, or participate in them. Large numbers of Old World citizens were employed by the pageants and their associated model settlements, which were living ethnological museums. In addition to their historical and entertainment value, the pageants provided a refuge for certain citizens having an atavistic lifestyle inclination.

IMMORTALITY   in the Milieu, does not refer to unending spiritual life but rather to an individual's possession of the self-rejuvenating genes that preclude death by old age. Such persons are, of course, subject to accidental death and to certain diseases. However, they often possess extraordinary powers of self-redaction, making them far less vulnerable to trauma or infection than ordinary mortals. The Remillard Family had the strongest reservoir of "immortality genes." Marc and his two children possessed the supradominant strain that was lost with the destruction of the Mental Man laboratories during the Rebellion. The founder of the original mutation in the Remillard Family was Donatien, Marc's great-grandfather. *See also* the Remillard Family Tree in this *Pliocene Companion*. Cf. REJUVINATION.

I-MODE   Milieu slang for the intimate mode of far-speech, telepathic communication directed at a single receiver with other minds excluded. An aritificial i-mode carrier is a mechanically augmented thought projection directed along the intimate mode, used between Grand Masters under circumstances that render ordinary i-mode communication difficult.

INERTIALESS DRIVER   the rho-field-generating mechanism of a subluminal starship or atmosphere flying machine. *See* Rho-Field.

INMAN, RONALD ex-Rebel at Ocala, the mate of Everett Garrison. Like him, he commanded a dreadnought in the Rebel Twelfth Fleet.

INTERVENTION, GREAT took place in 2013, when antimetapsychic sentiment was highest among "normal" humanity. Denis Remillard, his wife Lucille Cartier, and a group of several thousand imperfectly operant metas from all over the world gathered in New Hampshire, USA, in a last-ditch effort to fend off the ruin of their plans. Eluding a mob of armed antimeta fanatics, they fled to the top of Mount Washington and broadcast into outer space a concerted telepathic cry for help. (There had previously been hints that humanity was not the only rational race in our galaxy.) The almost immediate response to their plea was the Intervention: Hundreds of exotic spacecraft appeared simultaneously above the large population centers of Earth—as well as above Mount Washington— announcing the reality of the Galactic Milieu. Details of the Great Intervention are recapitulated in the first volume of the Milieu Trilogy, *Jack the Bodiless*.

IRENA *See* O'Malley, Irena.

IRON MAIDEN the largest of the Lowlife iron-mining villages of the Moselle River Valley. It suffered a vicious attack by Firvulag while Tony Wayland was resident.

IRON VILLAGES fortified Lowlife settlements established along the Moselle River following the Finiah battle, for the purpose of mining iron. The northerly cluster, in the vicinity of the modern Nancy, included Iron Maiden, Hematite, Mesabi, Haut-Fourneauville, and Vulcan. Fort Rusty, farther south upstream, was the principal metalworking establishment and supply depot.

ISKENDER-KERNONN LORD OF ANIMALS (eesh-ken-DAY'r kur-NAH'n) Tanu sobriquet bestowed upon

Iskender Karabekir, Turkish animal trainer responsible for domesticating chalikos, hellads, and amphicyons. He was given a golden torc and accorded high honor, even though he had no significant latent powers. Later, Lowlife spies under Madame Guderian set him up in ambush and he was slain by the Firvulag. Her role in this affair earned Madame a golden torc of her own, freshly plucked from the throat of the defunct Kernonn.

JACK THE BODILESS, SAINT *See* Remillard, Jon.

JACOBY, LEILA member of Ocala's second generation and wife to Chris Strangford. She was the mother of Joel Strangford and the daughter of Heather Jacoby.

JACOBY, HEATHER ex-Rebel at Ocala.

JAFAR, DR. physician of Finiah, released from silver-torc bondage by Lowlives after the fall of the city. He later worked among the Iron Villages.

JANGO a crust driller of Lisboa Metro, an associate of Stein Oleson.

JARROW, ALONZO ex-Rebel at Ocala, husband of Isobel Layton and father of Vaughn Jarrow.

JARROW, VAUGHN a member of Ocala's second generation, the most powerful farsensor among the Children of Rebellion. He was the first to notice the rising power of Felice Landry and played a pivotal role in the children's scheme to escape their elders. In spite of his talents, he was generally disliked because of his boorish habits and cruelty.

JEAN-PAUL a gray-torc assistant to Lady Epone at Castle Gateway when Group Green arrived.

JERRY a gold-torc human in Commander Congreve's guard force at Goriah.

JIRO a Lowlife of the Vale of Hyenas, killed by Firvulag while escorting Tony Wayland to Hidden Springs.

JOE-DON palace servitor at Roniah when Bryan Grenfell passed through on his way to the Tanu capital.

JOHNSON, DENNY a stalwart fighter of Hidden Springs and close associate of Chief Burke. In the Milieu he was a leading baritone with the Royal Opera at Covent Garden. He was born in New York City.

KAISERSTUHL (KY-zur-sh'tool)   an extinct volcano in the Rhine Graben near modern Frieburg. During the Pliocene, it was the site of the Tanu city of Finiah. A blast from the Spear of Lugonn caused lava to gush forth from it, destroying the city's barium mine. The literal meaning of the name is "King's Seat." It is interesting to note that Finiah was the Tanu capital in the early years of the Many-Colored Land.

KALIPIN THE BOGLE (KAH-lih-pin BOH-g'l)   a Howler of the Feldberg, sent by Sugoll to escort Madame Guderian's expedition to the mountain. Later, he was a guide of the Second Ship's Grave Expedition under Basil Wimborne. After that he guided the Fennoscandian operation.

KAMILDA (kuh-MIL-duh)   a farsensing female warrior of Finiah, present at the city's invasion.

KANDA-KANDA   a human dancer of renown in Muriah.

KANG LEE elite gold officer on the Monte Rosa Expedition.

KARBREE THE WORM (KAH'r-bree) a young Firvulag ogre and battle-champion, elevated to hero status on the field of the Last Grand Combat. He was "bumped" from the Heroic Encounters on a technicality. Later, he and his force ambushed the Lowlife squad under Orion Blue that was escorting Tony Wayland and Dougal to Hidden Springs. He captured Tony and took him to High Vrazel. Karbree was a protegé of the Dreadful Skathe and a member of the Gnomish Council until his death at Bardelask. His illusory aspect was that of a limbless dragon, the "worm" of European legend.

KARIN daughter of Isak Henning and the Firvulag hybrid woman Borghild, later mother of Huldah.

KAROLINA Lowlife of the Vale of Hyenas, killed while escorting Tony Wayand to Hidden Springs.

KATLINEL THE DARKEYED (KAT-lin-el) a hybrid High Table member, most junior of that body. She was Second Creator under Aluteyn until her elopement with Sugoll. Katlinel was the daughter of Leyr, banished ex-president of the Coercer Guild. As Sugoll's wife, she was Mistress of Nionel and Lady of the Howlers.

KAWAI, TADANORI (kah-wy-ee, tah-dah-nohree) called Old Man, in the Milieu, a prominent manufacturer of electronic equipment resident in Osaka, Japan. On a matter of principle he declined rejuvenation and came to the Many-Colored Land in late middle age to become a simple craftsman. He was Hidden Springs' expert in domestic manufactures. In the absence of Madame Guderian and Chief Burke, he served as Freeleader of the village.

KELOLO   gray-torc guardian at Castle Gateway during the arrival of Group Green.

KENDALL, TERESA   a powerful metapsychic of the Milieu, founder of the "bodiless" mutagene, who was married to Paul Remillard in 2037. Five of their eleven children survived to adulthood, including Marc and Jon Remillard. Her history is detailed in the first book of the Milieu Trilogy, *Jack the Bodiless. See also* the Remillard Family Tree in this *Pliocene Companion*.

KENNEDY, HUGHIE B., VII   major domo at Darask and senior servant to Lady Estella-Sirone. He prepared Black Crag for occupation by Elizabeth and her associates.

KEOGH, DIERDRE and DIARMID   twin brother and sister Rebels, also mates and the parents of Nial Keogh. They were an imperfect duality (q.v.) and the most powerful redactors in Marc Remillard's cabal. In the Milieu, they worked on the Mental Man project.

KEOGH, NIAL   member of Ocala's second generation, the son of Dierdre and Diarmid Keogh. He was a crafty, foxy-faced individual with strong coercive and creative powers; a crony of Hagen's, but generally mistrusted by his other contemporaries.

KERSIC, ISLE OF (KUR-sik)   name given to the Pliocene Mediterranean island that combined the masses of modern Corse and Sardegna. It was a home to certain Lowlife escapees from Aven, and periodically invaded by a Royal Flying Hunt. Isak Henning and Huldah lived there in a cave.

KHAN, KHALID (KAH'n, kah-LEED)   Lowlife of Hidden Springs, member of the village Steering Committee in charge of local industry, a metalsmith who later participated in the invasion of the torc works at Muriah.

KIKU (KEE-koo) Yosh Watanabe's chaliko. The name means "chrysanthemum."

KILO (KEE-loh) Milieu slang for kilogram, a unit of weight. Cf. KLOM.

KING, JOHN-HENRY gray-torc miner killed by Yotunag in Fennoscandia.

KING'S OWN ELITE GOLDS a guard force composed entirely of humans, under the direct command of King Aiken-Lugonn. Aiken originally promised a golden torc to any human who would pledge loyalty. When this proved impracticable, he reserved gold for the best fighters, technicians, and other specialists—whether genuinely latent or not. Many of the elite golds had been grays or silvers under the Tanu; but there were also barenecks who later wore gold, such as Yosh Watanabe. The golden torc conferred full citizenship upon a person. The elites enjoyed additional privileges, which they sometimes abused.

KIPOL GREENTEETH (KIH-pawl) a woodland Firvulag of Armorica, who waylaid Yosh Watanabe at a troll bridge near Goriah.

KLAHNINO, QUEEN (KLAH-nee-noh) wife to King Yeochee IV. The wife of the First Comer King Yeochee was also named Klahnino.

KLOM (kl'ahm) Milieu slang for kilometer, a unit of measure (which is pronounced kih-LAH-muh-tur in Standard English). Cf. Kilo.

KOLITEYR (KOH-lih-tey'r) a high-ranking farsensor in Finiah at the time of the invasion, killed by Chief Burke.

KONEYN (koh-NAY'n) in the Tanu language, "Land of Flowers," name given to the Iberian peninsula.

KOSTA   servitor at Castle Gateway during the arrival of Group Green.

KRAL (krah'l)   the great ceremonial cauldron of the Tanu Creator Guild, made of beaten gold, used in connection with Manifestations of Power. At the Grand Combat, the Kral was displayed to all and the Creator President was obliged to fill it "to the edification of the combatants." The vessel served to rescue Aiken and Mercy from the Flood. One may note that large bowls were a part of Celtic ritual, and the Celtic god Dagda had a cauldron of plenty. The name Kral or Graal is also given to a mystical vessel in Arthurian legends; but its origins antedate Christianity.

KRAMER, JORDAN   ex-Rebel at Ocala, former magnate of the Concilium, and a prominent psychophysicist. Together with Marc Remillard and Gerrit Van Wyk, he was a designer of the CE rig. During the Rebellion he designed other equipment to enhance the aggressive potential of Marc's anti-Milieu metaconcert. He was married to Margaret Ryerson in the Milieu and had three children. His first family was killed in the destruction of the Rebel planet Okanagon. In the Pliocene his wife was Audrey Truax, by whom he fathered Rebecca and Margaret Kramer.

KRAMER, MARGARET and REBECCA   members of Ocala's second generation, daughters of Jordan Kramer and Audrey Truax.

KRONDAKU (krah'n-DAH-koo), sing. & pl.; adj. KRONDAK   the second most ancient (after the Lylmik) of the coadunate Milieu races, having mercilessly logical minds and a grotesque and fearsome appearance, in which warts and tentacles are featured. They were the leading explorers and surveyors of the Milky Way Galaxy, ranging from the Hub to the Magellanic Clouds. Krondaku could endure a displacement factor, or "warp speed," of 370, the upper limit for Milieu races not using a cerebroenergetic enhancer. The Krondaku long took a dubious view of evolving humanity and voted against our admission to the Milieu. Later, during the Rebellion, they took melancholy satisfaction in saying, "We told you so." Metapsychic humans know that the Krondak bark is far worse than its bite; but "normal" humans are especially fearful of these hideous, superintelligent beings.

KUBANOCHOERUS (koo-bah'n-oh-KEE-rus) a giant swine whose fossils date from the Middle Miocene of the Caucasus; noted for having a single horn jutting from its forehead.

KUHAL EARTHSHAKER (KOO'ul) a member of the Host of Nontusvel, identical twin brother of Fian Skybreaker, under King Thagdal Second Lord Psychokinetic and High Table sitter. He was a close associate of Nodonn Battlemaster the head of the PK Guild, a doughty champion of the Tanu battle-company, and one of the Host leaders during the Last Grand Combat. Following the Flood he and Fian were cast away in Africa. After Fian's death, reduced to latency by grief and psychic trauma, he was cared for by Celadeyr. Cloud Remillard shared Kuhal's healing. When Nodonn returned, Kuhal joined the attack upon Aiken at Goriah. He was captured and punished following Nodonn's defeat, but later resumed his High Table seat under Aiken-Lugonn. He and Cloud Remillard became lovers and passed together through the reversed time-gate into the Milieu.

KUHSARN THE WISE (koo-SAH'rn) First Comer Firvulag, mentioned in Brede's Tale.

KWONG CHUN-MEI in the Milieu, a redactor and therapist on Denali, who worked in vain with the traumatized Elizabeth.

KYLLIKKI (kih-LEE-kee) a 70-meter four-masted schooner built by Walter Saastamoinen on Ocala Island. For a plan of the vessel, see "The Good Ship Kyllikki" in this *Pliocene Companion*. In the Finnish epic, *Kalevala*, Kyllikki is the young wife of the hero Lemminkainen, abandoned by her incurably adventure-seeking sailor-spouse.

LAAR (lah'r)   name given to the Pliocene Proto-Loire and Cher rivers. The name in the Tanu tongue means "Jungle River." The Laar was navigable from its mouth below Goriah to a stretch of rapids more than 400 km to the east, where the Western Track had its terminus. The Grove of May and the Tainted Swamp both lay near the mouth of the Laar.

LAMBALLE, GEORGES   father of Mercy, husband of Siobhan O'Connell, a resident of Brittany in the Old World.

LAMBALLE, MERCEDES called Mercy-Rosmar (roh'z-MAH'r)   formerly associate director of the Immersive Pageant at Riom, France. In the Many-Colored Land she was given a golden torc when the Tanu discovered her enormous latent creativity. After being impregnated by King Thagdal she was married to Nodonn Battlemaster and became Lady of Goriah. Eventually she challenged

Aluteyn for the presidency of the Creator Guild and won. Bryan Grenfell was her luckless human lover, who found in his femme fatale. Mercy was saved from the Flood by Aiken and later became his lover and co-conspirator as he schemed to usurp the Tanu throne. She gave birth to Thagdal's daughter Agraynel, then married Aiken at the Grand Loving. Aiken named her Queen when he assumed the throne. Mercy remained loyal in her heart to Nodonn; and when the Tanu Battlemaster reappeared, she conspired with him against Aiken. Aiken executed her for treason when she immobilized his cache of Milieu arms. Aiken subsumed Mercy's great metapsychic attributes as she died.

LANCING   a drastic redactive technique, involving release of pent-up psychic poisons in abrupt torrents. It is hazardous both for the patient and for the redactor.

LAND OF YOUTH   in Tanu legend, the sanctuary from Nightfall, from which the new, more perfect race would arise. One may compare it with the Celtic paradise Tír na nOg.

LANDRY, FELICE   a young athlete having enormous latent faculties of coercion, creativity, and psychokinesis. She was always mentally unbalanced and became an active psychopath after torture by Culluket—which also raised her powers to full operancy. Her aggressive metafunctions were perhaps the greatest ever manifest in a member of the human race. As an act of revenge she opened Gibraltar and initiated the Flood. Eventually Felice was involved in a titanic confrontation with the forces of Aiken and Marc Remillard at the Río Genil. Her very complex history is detailed in the first three volumes of the Saga of Pliocene Exile.

LANGSTONE   a Lowlife on the first iron-seeking expedition.

LAROCHE, GUY "BOOM-BOOM"   ex-Rebel of Ocala, a powerful coercer-creator, in the Milieu Marc Remillard's security chief and personal enforcer. He was a boyhood friend of Marc's from New Hampshire, noted for his quick temper and amorous conquests. In the Pliocene he fathered André Sherwoode-Laroche, Kané Fox-Laroche, Riki Teichman, and Davey Warshaw.

LARS   special-effects technician at the Grand Tourney, operator of the tug-of-war device.

LATENT   in metapsychology, refers to those metafunctions that cannot be used consciously by an individual—because of lack of training, inhibiting factors, trauma, or mind-blocks of uncertain origin. The converse of latent is operant. In theory, all humans are possessed of metafunctions, even though these may be hopelessly latent or extremely meager. *See* Operant.

LATTICE   in the New Universal Field Theory of the Milieu, a dimensional dynamic-field construct (which can only be expressed mathematically) generating one of the six primary manifestations forming the universe, or reality. One can speak in a general way of spatial lattices, temporal lattices, matter lattices, energy lattices, vital lattices, and mental lattices. The lattices may be combined, and may have sublattices. The nodal points of interacting lattices equate with process. The various aspects of reality are said to arise from nodal points of the meshed lattices and equate with "waves" traveling within the lattices. *See also* Dynamic Fields; Mind.

LAWRENCE, properly **LAWRENCE MALLORY**   husband and co-worker of Elizabeth Orme, killed in the crash of their egg on the planet Denali. Like his wife he was a Grand Master Farspeaker and Redactor.

LAURA, properly **LAURA BRUCE-OVERTON**   an ex-Rebel of Ocala, the mother of Phil Overton. She was a medical technician in the Mental Man project and later worked with the Keoghs in the Ocala medical establishment.

LAYTON, ISOBEL   ex-Rebel at Ocala, mother of Vaughn Jarrow, wife of Alonzo Jarrow.

LECOCQ, COMMANDER   a human operant gold, commandant of the Roniah garrison at the time of the Grand Tourney.

LEE   former lover of Skipper Highjohn on the planet Tallahatchie.

LEILANI-TEGVEDA THE FAIRBROWED (lay-ee-LAH-nee teg-VAY-duh)   a gold-torc human woman operant, a member of the Peace Faction at Black Crag.

LENE (leen)   birth-planet of Brede Shipspouse, one of the Duat daughter-worlds. It should be noted that the daughter-world populations were neither Tanu nor Firvulag, but had the genes of both nations as a result of longstanding mixed mating. The people of Lene were almost fully humanoid in appearance. Of ordinary stature, they were mostly latent metapsychics and wore golden torcs. *See also* Duat.

LEYR THE BRAVE (lay'r)   also called the Banished, former Lord Coercer and First Comer among the Tanu, deposed after a skirmish with Marc's arriving Rebels left him badly injured and unable to resist his rival, Gomnol. Leyr went into exile but returned after Gomnol's death to challenge Imidol for presidency of the Coercers. Leyr was father to the hybrid Katlinel the Darkeyed.

LIEM a silver-torc associate of Tony Wayland in Finiah prior to its invasion.

LIFE-OFFERING ritualized death by roasting or distillation in the Great Retort (q.v.), reserved for criminals, disgraced persons, mental burn-outs, and deposed Tanu nobility.

LILLESTROM, ARNE-ROLF ex-Rebel of Ocala, an electronics expert and psychic warfare specialist.

LIMBO, GRAY Milieu slang term for the hyperspatial matrix. Too close scrutiny of this "colorless color" by humans traveling through hyperspace could lead to madness. The hypertemporal matrix that time-travelers passed through was a subtly different kind of gray, unfortunately never the subject of Milieu study. *See* the fourth Appendix to *The Adversary* for a full discussion of travel through hyperspace.

LIQUICELL a resilient Milieu material used for padding, mattresses, and the like.

LISETTE a silver-torc associate of Tony Wayland in Finiah prior to its invasion.

LITTLE GREEN ARMY in the Firvulag Grand Loving celebration, a mob of small children dressed in leaf-coats who drive away any miscreants who attempt to steal the brides.

LITTLE PEOPLE *See* Firvulag.

LOGAN, GENEVIEVE wife to Claude Majewski, and his colleague. Together they undertook salvage paleontology on newly colonized planets of the Human Polity. After her death, Claude went to the Pliocene, where he buried her ashes.

LOMNOVEL BRAINBURNER (LAH'm-noh-vel) City-Lord of Sayzorask and member of King Aiken-Lugonn's High Table.

LONDINIUM a "British" planet of the Human Polity.

LONG FJORD before the Flood, name given to a channel linking the Southern Lagoon Estuary to the Great Brackish Marsh. It was not a true fjord, but rather a deep canyon cut through a dike of unconsolidated volcanic materials.

LOUIE in the Milieu, proprietor of Chez Louis, a café near the Col de la Luère, west of Lyon, where Richard and Stein had their last meal before entering l'Auberge du Portail.

LOWLIFE pejorative applied to outlaw humans by the Tanu and Firvulag—adopted proudly by those same free-living people. To the Firvulag, *all* humans were Lowlives beneath honorable consideration. One could lie to them or break one's promises without incurring the ill will of the Goddess. The Tanu used the term for humans who ran away or otherwise defied their authority.

LOW MÊLÉE a preliminary event in the Grand Combat, which in the earliest days featured novice Tanu and Firvulag fighters. Later it featured only humans.

LUCIEN a Lowlife hunter of wild game at Hidden Springs.

LUGONN (loo-GAH'n) 1. Bright Lugonn or Lugonn the Shining was Tanu battlemaster in the abortive Nightfall War in the Duat Galaxy. He was the chosen royal heir, beloved of Mayvar Kingmaker. After the arrival on Pliocene Earth, he sacrificed himself in the Great Ordeal (q.v.) at the Ship's Grave. His skeleton in armor was discovered by Madame Guderian's expedition. Later, the flyer containing his remains was sunk in the crater lake by Basil's Bastards. 2. The name Lugonn was bestowed upon Aiken Drum by Mayvar after his defeat of Pallol One-Eye at the Last Grand Combat. He was called Aiken-Lugonn thereafter by Tanu and Firvulag. *See* Drum, Aiken.

LUKTAL (LOO'k-tah'l)   Tanu musician and worthy of the Creator Guild.

LULO (LOO-loh)   Firvulag concubine to King Yeochee IV.

LUSATIA   a "French" planet of the Human Polity.

LYLMIK (LIL-mik) pl. & sing.   the oldest and least numerous race of the Galactic Milieu, mysterious in their actions as well as their origins. Krondak legends say that the Lylmik date from the previous universe—i.e., from before the Big Bang, which they somehow managed to survive. Poltroyan legends say that the Lylmik rehabilitated their dying sun, a red giant, turning it into a G3 by a metapsychic infusion of fresh hydrogen, transmuted from an unknown energy source. The poetical Gi believe that the Lylmik are pseudocorporeal messengers of the Cosmic All. The bumptious Simbiari don't know what to make of the Lylmik, but distrust them because they show an obvious bias toward humanity, having been the prime movers of the Intervention. Humans suspect that the Lylmik—whose forms are only partially visible to the naked eye and the deep-seeing eye—are extragalactic in origin and almost entirely "mental" in nature. The Lylmik themselves absent-mindedly declare that they don't know where they came from or what their true nature might be—and why should the other races be concerned when the Lylmik themselves are not? Humans are bemused by all this, but nevertheless esteem the Lylmik above all other coadunate races because it is obvious that the mysterious entities love humanity and are determined to shepherd our metapsychic evolution until we fulfill our immense potential. The human-Lylmik connection is detailed in the Milieu Trilogy.

MABINO DREAMSPINNER (muh-BEE-noh) First Comer Firvulag, artisan member of the Gnomish Council, and wife to Finoderee.

MACDONALD, DOROTHEA *See* Diamond Mask.

MACHAIRODUS (muh-KY-roh-dus) the genus of widespread Pliocene sabertooth cats, whose fossils have been found in most parts of the Northern Hemisphere. The European form, M. aphanistus, was about the size of a modern lion, with canines some 10 cm long that protruded from the mouth when the jaws were closed. I have arbitrarily given these animals the lovely coat pattern of the clouded leopard, Panthera nebulosa, a modern jungle cat with primitive characteristics.

MAC SUIBHNE, SEUMAS (mak SWEE-nee, SHAY-mus) a technician among Basil's Bastards, suspected of plotting theft of a flying machine.

MACSWEENEY a ring-hockey player on Acadie, savaged by Felice.

MADAME *See* Guderian, Angélique.

MAGGERS nom d'exil of an elite gold on the Bardelask expedition.

MAGISTRATUM the law enforcement and judicial arm of the Galactic Milieu. Administered on its highest levels by forensic redactors, the Magistratum is fully capable of ascertaining the motivation—and guilt—of malefactors through direct scrutiny of minds. There is no appeal from the decisions of the Magistratum, but its judgments and corrections are on the most part humane and equitable to perpetrator and victim alike. Operation of the Magistratum is described in the Milieu Trilogy.

MAGLARN WRINKLE-MEAT (MAG-lah'rn) defunct Firvulag hero, once an antagonist of King Thagdal.

MAGNATE title given to those Grand Master metapsychics serving on the Concilium of the Galactic Milieu. In theory, the magnates of all six coadunate races had an equal status. In practice the Lylmik exerted the greatest power because of their ancient wisdom. Paul Remillard, father of Marc and Jon, was the first human magnate.

MAGNUS *See* Bell, Magnus.

MAJEWSKI, CLAUDE (muh-JES-kee) his own North American pronunciation—paleontologist and member of Group Green, the husband of Genevieve Logan. He became a close friend of Sister Amerie. His adventures are detailed in *The Many-Colored Land* and *The Golden Torc*. The Majewskis are a venerable Polish house allied to the Starykon clan. The arms are gules, a horse forcene argent, engirthed sable.

MALACHEE (MAH'l-uh-chee)   Firvulag taverner, proprietor of Malachee's Toot near Goriah.

MALIETOA (mah-lee-ay-TOH-uh)   male silver-torc Polynesian attendant at the Calamosk baths.

MANAPOURI (mah-nah-po'OO-ree)   a "New Zealander" planet in the Human Polity.

MANCHINEEL BAY (MAN-chih-neel)   an inlet on the southern end of Ocala Island. See the Maps of Ocala in this *Pliocene Companion*. It was named by a homesick ex-Rebel after a noted Milieu resort. The manchineel tree, which grew abundantly around this bay, has extremely poisonous sap; even water dripping from the leaves can cause skin irritation.

MANETTI, ALDO   technician and mountain climber among Basil's Bastards.

MANION, ALEXIS   ex-Rebel of Ocala, a brilliant dynamic-field researcher specializing in mental lattices. He was a boyhood friend of Marc Remillard and one of the leading lights of the Rebellion. Manion was the chief promoter of the thesis that Unity would endanger the individuality of the human race, a philosophical basis for the Rebellion—especially among nonmetas, who were encouraged to believe that humanity would be "swallowed" and dominated by exotics if the Milieu loyalists had their way. In the Pliocene, Manion changed his mind. He fathered a daughter, Diane, and saw her become the intimate of Marc's son, Hagen. Manion was responsible for converting Ocala's second generation away from Marc's Mental Man scheme. As a result, he was confined to a docilator much of the time. His Pliocene adventures are detailed in *The Nonborn King* and *The Adversary*; and he is also a principal character in the Milieu Trilogy. *See also* Guderian Tau-field Generator.

MANION, DIANE   member of Ocala's second generation, the daughter of Alexis Manion and mate of Hagen Remillard. Her prime metafunction was psychokinesis.

MANY-COLORED LAND   in the Tanu language, taynel o pogekône, the name given by Brede and the exotic First Comers to Pliocene Earth—especially Europe, where they settled. It is interesting to note that the ancient Celts used this term (in Gaelic, Tír Ildathach), for their paradise. Cf. LAND OF YOUTH.

MARCHAND, ROY   ex-Rebel of Ocala, a former military aide to Walter Saastamoinen, he became first mate of the Kyllikki.

MARIALENA   *See* Torrejon, Marialena.

MARSHAK, MOE   a gray-torc soldier at the battle of Finiah.

MARSHAL OF SPORT   *See* Heymdol Buccinator.

MARTHA   a former field-generator engineer impressed into the Tanu breeding program, who escaped from Finiah and lived at Hidden Springs. She accompanied Madame Guderian's expedition to the Ship's Grave and helped render the Spear and a flyer operational. Martha became the lover of Richard Voorhees.

MARY-DEDRA (DEE-druh)   the Tanu sobriquet of Maribeth Kelly-Dakin, gold-torc operant, farsensor, and a confidant of Mayvar Kingmaker. She was an ineffective guard of Stein Oleson. After the Flood, she attached herself to Elizabeth, seeing to domestic arrangements during the exodus from Aven. She became executive housekeeper at Black Crag and bore a black-torc hybrid son of King Thagdal, Brendan.

MASSEUSE, LA a mechanical massage device much used in the Milieu.

MASTERCLASS adjective usually referring to the higher classes of metapsychics. *See* Grand Master.

MATIWILDA *See* Shaunavon, Matiwilda.

MATSU common abbreviation for the Matsushita RL-9 or similar red-laser weapons. *See* Zapper.

MAXL Lowlife inhabitant of Hidden Springs, the subject of successful psychotherapy by Sister Amerie.

MAYVAR KINGMAKER (may-VAH'r) First Comer and President of the Farsensor Guild. By ancient privilege she had the right to select the Tanu kings through a love-test. Having chosen Thagdal, then nominated Bright Lugonn (who, however, died at the Ship's Grave), she had reluctantly settled for Nodonn as Number Three when Aiken showed up. Mayvar was a secret member of the Peace Faction. Except for Brede, she was the oldest exotic on Pliocene Earth, age 3352 of our years.

MCGILLICUDDY, YUGGOTH elite gold electronics technician on the Río Genil expedition.

MEADOW MOUNTAIN *See* Feldberg.

MEDOR (MEE-doh'r) Great Captain and battle-champion of the Firvulag, a First Comer who was promoted to battlemaster under Sharn and Ayfa. In the Last Grand Combat he fought to a tie with Kuhal Earthshaker in the Heroic Encounters. He served as sponsor-brother to young Sharn-Ador. His wife was Andamathe.

MEGAHIPPUS alias Hypohippus, a three-toed forest horse of the North American Pliocene, about the size of a rhino. Specimens were brought to Ocala by the ex-Rebels as novelties.

MEGAPOD   common Milieu name for *Gigantopithecus megapodius*, also called sasquatch, bigfoot, or yeti, a huge anthropoid native to the dense forests of North America, the uplands of Nepal, Xizang, the Pamir and Tien Shan ranges, and certain other parts of the world. Raimo Hakkinen worked in the Megapod Reserve of British Columbia, famous as the birthplace of Jack the Bodiless.

MEGOWAN, COACH   executive of a ring-hockey team, the Greenhammers, on Acadie. He was Felice's boss.

MELINA   human laboratory assistant to Greg-Donnet in Nionel.

MENTAL MAN   a concept developed by Marc Remillard, the beginning implementation of which was guided by Jeffrey Steinbrenner and Dierdre and Diarmid Keogh. It theorized that the ultimate goal of human evolution was a bodiless brain capable of metapsychically generating any body form it chose—or none. Marc based the idea upon his observation of the sublethal mutation of his brother Jon, called Jack the Bodiless. Marc's scheme for the artificial engendering of Mental Man was utterly opposed by the exotic races of the Milieu and by the human Milieu-loyalists. The project, along with the more subtle opposition to Unity, became a prime cause of the Rebellion.

MERCY-ROSMAR   *See* Lamballe, Mercedes.

MERMELSTEIN, SAUL   *See* Burke, Peopeo Moxmox.

MESABI (meh-SAH-bee)   one of the Lowlife Iron Villages of the Moselle River.

METACONCERT a joint, harmonious action by numbers of meshed operant minds. When true synergy is attained, the concert yields a metapsychic output greater than the sum of the individual input energies. Efficient metaconcert requires sophisticated programming. Metaconcert should not be confused with Unity (q.v.).

METAFUNCTION informally called metability, mindpower, etc., is a high mental operation involving the interaction of mental lattices with other principal aspects of reality to yield phenomena not dependent upon physical causation. The main metafunctions are farsensing, coercion, creativity, psychokinesis, and redaction (qq.v.), which form the basis of Milieu metapsychology. Less well understood and rarer metafunctions include prolepsis or precognition, bilocation, d-jumping or teleportation, déjà vu, synchronicitous phenomena such as the influencing of future events, and "cosmic consciousness." The metafunctions, like the lower-mind functions, must usually be developed through training. At the time of the Great Intervention, most of humanity possessed latent (unusable) metafunctions; only a few thousand were operant (able to manifest their metafunctions at will and control them). All five of the exotic Milieu races are metafunctionally operant; humanity was in the process of becoming so when it was admitted to the Milieu. Among the many terms that have been applied to metafunctions are psi, ESP, paranormal events, psychic phenomena, altered states of consciousness, psychoenergetics, bioenergetics, parapsychological effects, miracles, and magic. *See also* Metapsychology.

METAPSYCHIC COMPLEXUS the "blueprint" of total metapsychic function contained within an individual mind. It is the complexus that is susceptible to subsumption (q.v.), not the true personality or individual mind.

METAPSYCHOLOGY   the science studying the inter-action of mind (mental dynamic-field lattices) and the physical processes; also, the study of mind's place in the universe, especially as manifested in the metafunctions. The pre-Intervention pioneers of metapsychology include William James, Sigmund Freud, C. G. Jung, Pierre Teil-hard de Chardin, J. B. Rhine and Louisa E. Rhine, Charles T. Tart, Lawrence LeShan, I. M. Kogan, Viktor Ada-menko, and Gardner Murphy—among others.

MEVA (MEE-vuh)   a coercer associate of Gomnol at Coercer House.

MEYN THE UNSLEEPING (mah'n)   Tanu redactor at Black Crag, a member of the Peace Faction.

MIAKONN HEALERSON (mee-uh-KAH'n)   City-Lord of Var-Mesk, a son of Dionket; his mind was destroyed by Culluket after an attack upon Aiken-Lugonn.

MILIEU   *See* Galactic Milieu.

MILIEU TRILOGY   the books *Jack the Bodiless*, *Diamond Mask*, and *Magnificat*, works in progress at the time of this *Companion's* writing. They detail the events following the Great Intervention, up to and including the Metapsychic Rebellion.

MIMEE (MIH-mee)   a stalwart dwarf Firvulag, Viceroy of Famorel and member of the Gnomish Council. His illusory aspect was a great flightless bird.

MINANONN THE PROUD (MIH-nun-nah'n), called HERETIC, or MINANONN OF THE THREEFOLD FUNCTION   a Tanu First Comer, son of Thagdal by Queen Boanda in the Duat Galaxy. He was chosen bat-tlemaster after the demise of Bright Lugonn and served for some 500 years. After declaring against the battle-religion during the Times of Unrest he was challenged and defeated by Nodonn. Minanonn and other members of the militant Peace Faction chose exile rather than life-offering in the Great Retort. They lived first in the wilderness of northern Koneyn and latterly in the Pyrénées. Minanonn was primarily a coercer, but his PK and creativity were also formidable. His emblem was the triskelion, symbolic of his three great powers. After the Flood, Minanonn became a close friend to Elizabeth and aided her on several occasions.

MIND   1. An individual's interaction with the mental lattices of reality; that part of a living organism that manifests itself through the brain—feeling, perceiving, willing, thinking, reasoning, and reflecting upon itself; psyche, spirit, or soul; the nonmaterial part of a sapient entity. An individual mind grows but does not evolve. It is brought into being, but most Milieu theoreticians believe that it cannot be annihilated. 2. The collective consciousness of a planet or galaxy, usually capitalized as Mind. Some researchers (viz. Teilhard de Chardin) have called it the noösphere or integrated planetary consciousness. It embraces not only sapient beings but also lower orders of consciousness in animals, plants, and substances only minimally interacting with the mental lattices. It is believed that once a planet attains a certain population of rational beings, a World Mind will have its "noögenesis," just as life early had its "biogenesis" and the planet itself had a "geogenesis." The most primitive aspect of a developing planetary Mind is rapid communication among poulation groups (the communication network being analogous to the nervous system of a higher animal), resulting in an atmosphere of racial solidarity or "brotherhood." Further evidence of a gestating World Mind is an accelerated "knowledge explosion" and a shared technoeconomy. Then comes the spread of metafunctional operancy, ultimately resulting in coadunation (q.v.), which can be compared to the development of sapience in an animal.

The Galactic Mind embraces all coadunate, noncoadunate, living, and nonliving creatures interacting with the mental lattices. Milieu theoreticians do not equate the Galactic Mind (or even the larger Universal Mind that might exist in the future) with God, who is perceived as an All in all in which all Mind lives and moves and has its being. (Cf. Acts 17:28.) *See* Unity, and, for some source materials, the Bibliography in this *Pliocene Companion.*

MISHIMA, ALAN　counselor at l'Auberge du Portail.

MITHEYN (mih-THAY'n)　City-Lord of Sasaran, Host member, killed in an early encounter of the Tanu with Marc Remillard's Rebels.

MITIGATOR　a mental program originated by the living Ships of the Duat Galaxy that moderates or entirely eliminates the pain that sentient entities usually suffer when passing through an upsilon-field gateway into hyperspace. Brede had the mitigator as a legacy from her Spouse, but chose not to use it when undergoing her elevation to operancy by Elizabeth. Passengers on the Ships routinely made use of the mitigator. Among the Tanu, the Redactor Guild were custodians of the mitigator program, even though it no longer seemed to have a practical application in the Many-Colored Land.

MODUPLEX (MAH'd-oo-plex)　a compact, programmable manufacturing device of the Milieu, producing various types of consumer goods. The most common types made clothing, footgear, domestic linens, paper products, cosmetics, and mixed drinks. They use either recycled or fresh raw materials. Many Milieu householders had a number of devices; they were also for rent by the hour in municipal moduplex centers. To utilize a clothing moduplex, a client simply inserted a program, fabric, and notions, and a custom-made item was delivered ready to wear.

MONOLOKEE THE SCUNNERSOME (mah-nuh-LOH-kee) an ogre officer under the command of Betularn of the White Hand.

MONTAGNE NOIRE (moh'n-TAH'ng'y n'WAH'r) an ancient upland region in southern France. Geologists use the term to embrace several ranges of low mountains or hills in the vicinity of the city of Castres. *See* Black Crag.

MOREYN GLASSCRAFTER (moh-RAY'n) Tanu creator of Var-Mesk, the artisan who crafted Nodonn's glass armor. He was appointed City-Lord by Aiken-Lugon following the treason of Miakonn. He assisted Nodonn in his comeback attempt. His wife was Glanluil.

MORGENTHALER, JILLIAN a member of Ocala's second generation, a PK adept and boatbuilder, daughter of Eileen Morgenthaler. She was the skipper of the ketch that carried the first small expedition of Cloud Remillard to Spain to negotiate with Felice.

MORIGEL (MOH-ree-gel) in the mythology of Duat, a portent of Nightfall, a monstrous black carrion-eating bird. The name can be translated "raven." Felice used the nom de guerre Phyllis-Morigel on the way to the torc works in Muriah.

MORNA-IA (MOR-nuh EE-uh) a First Comer, a powerful farsensor who was appointed president of that guild by Aiken-Lugonn, thus becoming ex-officio Kingmaker. She was saved from the Flood by Alberonn, together with her daughter-in-law Eadnar. The prolepsis of Morna-Ia foresaw that Mercy's infant daughter Agraynel would become the next queen of the Many-Colored Land.

MOUNT OF HEROES eminence west of Muriah, crowned by twin crags, originally named the Mount of Lugonn and Sharn by First Comers. The College of Redactors was situated on the southeastern slope, and the guild owned the entire mountain by express command of Brede. It was a refuge during the Flood. In Milieu times, the mountain was called Monte del Toro, at 400 meters the highest point on the island of Menorca.

MULDOWNY, CYNDIA wife to Marc Remillard and mother of Hagen and Cloud. She was killed by Marc shortly before the climax of the Metapsychic Rebellion. A distant relative of the Remillards, she also carried the famous immortality gene. Her history is detailed in the third volume of the Milieu Trilogy, *Magnificat*.

MULHACÉN, MOUNT (mool-ah-THAY'n or mool-ah-SAY'n) —the first pronunciation being the classic one, the second Standard English—a mountain in the Sierra Nevada of southern Spain, elevation during the Milieu 3478 meters, the highest peak in Europe outside of the Alps or Caucasus. During the Pliocene it was higher. Felice had her lair on its slope.

MULTNOMAH an "American" planet in the Human Polity.

MURIAH (myoo-RY-uh) Tanu capital city, situated on the tip of the Aven Peninsula above the White Silver Plain. It was a working administrative center containing the headquarters of the five Guilds Mental and the palace of the sovereign. The name means "White City." It was devastated by the Flood and abandoned.

NARNIA   a faerytale kingdom featured in C. S. Lewis's juvenile series, The Chronicles of Narnia.

NAZIR (nah-ZEER)   a rhocraft engineer and member of Basil's Bastards who participated in the final assault upon Monte Rosa.

NEBULIN   a sparkling luxury fabric of the Milieu.

NEURAL BATH   a more or less continuous ameliorative effort by a redactor, especially one generated by peripheral-mode activity.

NEUSTRIA   a "French" plant in the Human Polity.

NEW SEA   name given to the body of water in the Mediterranean Basin of the Pliocene, after the Flood.

NEW UNIVERSAL FIELD THEORY   *See* Universal Field Theory.

NEYAL THE YOUNGER (nay'l) City-Lord of Sasaran after the Flood and a member of Aiken-Lugonn's High Table.

NIGHTFALL WAR in the battle-religion of Duat as practiced by the Tanu and Firvulag, an apocalyptic conflict "when the earth shall be torn asunder, and high heaven." Nightfall was a true Ragnarok concept, the end of the Duat world, which would engender a "new and more perfect people" arising from the ruins. Following Night, the twin aspects of the Goddess, Tana and Té, "shall be sisters no more but one," as it was in the beginning. The reactionary Tanu and Firvulag of Duat, defying the more progressive federation of daughter-worlds, practiced the outlawed battle-religion and actively sought to initiate Nightfall. Driven to the edge of their home galaxy, the remnant of fanatics planned to bring on Nightfall by fighting each other to the death, but were persuaded by Brede to emigrate to the Many-Colored Land. The resurgence of the Nightfall concept on Pliocene Earth is detailed in the last two books of the Saga. *See also* Goddess; Peace Faction.

NINELVA (nih-NEL-vuh) female coercer slain by the human force invading the torc factory.

NIONEL (NY-uh-nel) a great city of the Firvulag on the Nonol River, adjacent to the Field of Gold. It was abandoned during the years that the Tanu dominated the Grand Combat, but rehabilitated when turned over to the Howlers by Sharn and Ayfa. Nionel (the name means "City of Gold") was built of yellow stone and had gilded domed towers. It was connected to the fighting ground across the river by a Rainbow Bridge.

NIRUPAM (NEE-roo-pah'm) Sherpa artisan among Basil's Bastards.

NODONN BATTLEMASTER (noh-DAH'n) oldest son of King Thagdal and Queen Nontusvel, leader of the Host, Battlemaster of the Tanu, President of the Psychokinetic Guild, and City-Lord of Goriah. His metapsychic prowess was without peer among the Tanu. He possessed all five metafunctions and utilized them to spectacular effect. Because of his impaired reproductive capacity, Nodonn was only reluctantly named heir apparent to the Tanu throne by Mayvar Kingmaker. (The Tanu King was traditionally chosen for his superior germ plasm.) Some 800 years old, Nodonn married Mercy-Rosmar, originally with the motive that her tremendous creativity would help him to beget powerful offspring. (Only a few "languid daughters" survived of his earlier liaisons.) Soon he loved Mercy with heartfelt passion, which she returned. As Battlemaster of the Grand Combat victors, Nodonn was custodian of the Sword of Sharn, the Combat trophy. He retained it when he was cast away on Kersic during the Flood. Ultimately he confronted Aiken-Lugonn in a duel, in which he utilized the Sword and his own great mental powers. Nodonn's heraldic cognizance was a smiling sun-face. His history is detailed in the first three books of the Saga.

NONOL (NOH-nawl) a watercourse of the Hercynian Forest, analogous to the Proto-Yonne. Burask lay on its upper reaches and Nionel farther downstream. The confluence of the Nonol with the Seekol, or Proto-Seine, was just below Nionel. The name means "Golden River."

NONTUSVEL OF THE HOST, QUEEN (NAH'n-toos-vel) third wife, after Boanda and Anéar-Ia, and queen consort of Thagdal. She was a First Comer, but married the King after the Tanu arrived on Pliocene Earth. Her predecessors had proved largely infertile, due to solar radiation. Nontusvel's brood, the notorious Host, numbered 242. It included Nodonn, Culluket, Kuhal and Fian, Imidol, Riganone, Epone, and Velteyn of Finiah. The

Queen was a gentle but relentless soul. Her primary meta-faculties were coercion, redaction, and psychokinesis, but she was powerfully creative and farsensitive as well.

NOVO JANEIRO a "Brazilian" planet of the Human Polity.

NOWAK, STOSH gray-torc miner in Fennoscandia, killed by Yotunag.

NUCKALARN (NUH'k-uh-lah'rn) adolescent Firvulag hostler at Malachee's Toot.

NUCKALAVEE THE SKINLESS (nuk-uh-LAH-vee) ogre, battle-champion of the Firvulag whose illusory aspect was that of a gigantic flayed centaur. He distinguished himself in the sack of Finiah and was later slain during the Last Grand Combat.

OCALA ISLAND (oh-KAH-lah) name given by the ex-Rebels to Pliocene Florida in North America, which at that time was a large island separated from the mainland by Apalachee Channel. For maps, see pp. 212 and 213 in this *Pliocene Companion*. The survivors of the Metapsychic Rebellion lived on Ocala for twenty-seven years following their arrival in the Pliocene.

OCHAL THE HARPER (OKH'l) Tanu farsensor stalwart, grandson of Armida of Bardelask who led the unsuccessful relief expedition to that city. He was one of Aiken's deputies at Goriah and later was named to his High Table as titular City-Lord of abandoned Bardelask. Ochal's heraldic cognizance was a golden harp. He was in charge of base operations on Monte Rosa.

O'CONNELL, SIOBHAN (shuh-VAW'n) mother of Mercy Lamballe and wife to Georges Lamballe.

OGMOL (AH'g-mawl) hybrid creator, a son of King Thagdal, assigned by him to assist Bryan Grenfell in an anthropological survey of Tanu-human relations. He was later killed by order of the King.

OGRE name given to gigantic Firvulag individuals.

OKANAGON (oh-kuh-NAH-gun) a cosmopolitan planet of the Human Polity, Sector Base and home of the Twelfth Fleet, whose dirigent was Patricia Castellane. A Rebel stronghold, it was devastated during the Metapsychic Rebellion.

OLAR ZEALATRIX (oh-LAH'r) novice-mistress of the College of Redactors who took Sukey Davies in charge.

OLD ONES in many of Earth's mythologies, the name given to a (generally) humanoid race resident upon the planet prior to the advent of humanity.

OLESON, CARY mother of Stein Oleson, tragically killed during his childhood.

OLESON, STEIN a member of Group Green, he was a planet crust driller assigned to the Lisboa Power Grid repair crew. He entertained fantasies of Viking life. In the Pliocene, Stein married Sukey Davies and assisted Felice in the opening of the Gibraltar Gate. After the Flood, he and Sukey and their infant son Thor lived in an isolated cabin in the Bordeaux Estuary. Stein's adventures are told in the first two volumes of the Saga.

OLONE (oh-LOH'n) coercer maiden of Calamosk, later wife to Sullivan-Tonn, the daughter of Onedan Trumpeter. She became infatuated with Aiken and had ambitions of becoming his queen.

OLTAAR (oh'l-TAH'r) a tributary of the Baar, analogous to the Proto-Lot. Its name means "Cascade River."

O'MALLEY, ARKADY PETROVICH "ARKY" ex-Rebel of Ocala and boyhood friend of Marc Remillard who became an officer in the Rebel starship armada. He was the father of Irena O'Malley.

O'MALLEY, IRENA a member of Ocala's second generation, daughter of Arkady O'Malley. She was the mate of Veikko Saastamoinen.

OMININ-LIMPIROTIN (OH-mih-nin lim-PEER-oh-tin) Fourth Interlocutor of the Concilium, a distinguished citizen of the Poltroyan Polity.

ONEDAN TRUMPETER (OH-nee-dah'n) before the Flood, City-Lord of Calamosk. He was father of Olone and responsible for her engagement to Sullivan-Tonn.

ONE-HANDED WARRIOR a portent of Nightfall in Duat mythology.

ONION RIVER a watercourse debouching into the eastern Lac de Bresse, analogous to the modern Ognon. There was a gray-torc fort at its mouth guarding the Finiah Track through the Belfort Gap.

OOKPIK nom d'exil of Ransome B. Harp, an Inuit engineer of Alaska, USA, a member of Basil's Bastards who participated in the final assault on Monte Rosa.

OPENING OF THE SKY an ancient opening ceremony of the Grand Combat, involving the dissipation of clouds by means of the laserlike Sword and Spear. The Sword alone was used for most of the exotic sojourn on Pliocene Earth, since the Spear was left at the Ship's Grave with the body of Bright Lugonn.

OPERANT in metapsychology, refers to those meta-functions that are available for controlled use by an individual mind. Its converse is latent. In the Pliocene, the Tanu latents were rendered imperfectly operant by their golden torcs. The daughter-races of Duat also used torcs. In the Milieu, humans first became reliably operant through "bootstrap" self-training, without mechanical aids, in the late twentieth and early twenty-first centuries. After the Intervention, Milieu educational techniques, administered by human preceptors and commencing in utero, were used to train natural operants. Operants constituted a small but increasing percentage of the largely latent human population.

ORCADIA a cosmop world of the Human Polity having a rather cold climate; famous for wool products.

OREOPITHECUS a genus of long-armed ape, type of the family Oreopithecidae, having the general appearance of a slender chimpanzee. It had certain hominid characteristics in its teeth and walked upright as well as swinging by its arms. It was a dweller in wet forests. Oreopithecus was abundant in the Upper Miocene. The specimens living around Monte Rosa were already a relict population whose niche was being taken over by Ramapithecus.

ORGANIC MIND in the Saga, a term applied to the most efficient kind of metaconcert. It should not be confused with a World or Planetary Mind, although some nonfiction authors use the terms synonymously. *See also* Mind; Metaconcert.

ORISSA an "Indian" planet of the Human Polity, settled largely by Hindus.

ORME, ELIZABETH a member of Group Green who was a Grand Master Redactor and Farspeaker in the Milieu until most of her brain was destroyed in an accident.

When she was regenerated, she found herself reduced to latency, and this prompted her departure to the Pliocene. The shock of temporal translation began the restoration of her operant metafunctions. Elizabeth's husband, Lawrence Mallory, was killed in the accident that originally wiped out her powers. Her inability to come to terms with his death seems to have been the source of her metapsychic and emotional dysfunctions. Her adventures are detailed in the four books of the Saga.

OSGEYR (AH'z-gay'r)   City-Lord of Burask, killed in the Firvulag takeover. He was the brother to Bormol of Roniah and had a secret cache of Milieu weaponry that fell into the hands of the Firvulag.

OUROBOUROS   *See* page 220 for description.

OVERTON, CALINDA   member of Ocala's third generation, four-year-old daughter of Phil Overton.

OVERTON, PHIL   a member of Ocala's second generation, a close friend of Hagen Remillard and a leader in the trek from Africa to Europe. He was strong in PK and creativity. He was the son of Laura Bruce-Overton.

PALLOL ONE-EYE (PAY-lawl) Firvulag First Comer and battlemaster, whose immense creativity was manifested in a beam of psychoenergy projected from his left eye, usually shuttered by a patch. Pallol sulked and refused to lead the battle-company during the Tanu domination of the Grand Combat, delegating the task to Sharn-Mes. He was persuaded to return after the fall of Finiah. In the Last Grand Combat he dueled with Aiken in the Encounter of Battlemasters.

PARADISE RIVER a Pliocene stream draining out of the Black Forest, a tributary of the Rhine debouching near Finiah. It had its source in subterranean springs of the Feldberg. The Paradise may be analogous to the modern river of the Höllental, near Freiburg.

PARIS BASIN a swampy lowland region at the northern edge of the Hercynian Forest, drained by the Nonol River and other tributaries of the Seekol. It was a refuge of Lowlives, who dwelt there in stilt-villages.

PARTHOL SWIFTFOOT (PAH'r-th'l) condemned murderer among the Tanu, who escaped in the floating Retort and became City-Lord of Calamosk after the death of Aluteyn.

PEACE FACTION formally, the Fellowship of the Mother of Peace, a Tanu group opposed to the battle-religion. It was founded by Mayvar, Minanonn, and Dionket several hundred years after the exotic advent upon Pliocene Earth, when the futility of the Grand Combat was becoming increasingly obvious. Its efforts were clandestine until Minanonn underwent a moral crisis and refused to continue in the role of battlemaster. The result was a brief civil war known as the Times of Unrest, squelched by Nodonn, as champion of King Thagdal and guardian of the battle-faith. Minanonn was driven into exile, along with certain of his followers. Dionket, Mayvar, and others remained within the Tanu Kingdom, continuing their secret conversion efforts. Minannon's enclave in the Pyrénées eventually gave refuge to Firvulag peace-lovers as well as Tanu. The religious beliefs of the Peace Faction were close to those of the Duat daughter-worlds. *See* Goddess; Battle-Religion.

PEGLEG *See* Fitharn Pegleg.

PELON-SU-KADAFIRON (PEH-lah'n soo kuh-DAF-uh-rah'n) a planet of the Poltroyan Polity.

PENNAR-IA (PEH'n-ah'r EE-uh) wife to Celadeyr of Afaliah.

PENNY, PENCE the minimum monetary unit of the Human Polity, the hundredth part of a dollar. *See also* Buck.

PEO. *See* Burke, Peopeo Moxmox.

PEPPINO aged gooseherd at Hidden Springs.

PEREDEYR FIRSTCOMER (peh'r-uh-DAY'r) redactor at Black Crag and member of the Peace Faction.

PERIPHERAL-MODE METAFUNCTION also called "dissociation," an apparent "splitting" of the mind so that one or more metafunctions operate independently of the others, or automatically, without continuing conscious volition. The farsenses most typically operate in peripheral mode (as when Marc monitored the region about the Río Genil, watching for Felice). PK and redaction may operate conjointly and peripherally during certain healing exercises, such as the neural bath. A therapist can be trained to exude redactive impulses while simultaneously attending to other duties—or healing more than one patient. The Tanu activation of faerie lights was a creative peripheral action undertaken by "lamplighters" among the exotics, who automatically broadcast surplus mental energies to the psychosensitive microbes inside the lamps, triggering bioluminescence.

PERKIN Lowlife vintner at Hidden Springs.

PHILEMON Lowlife architect of Hidden Springs, member of the village Steering Committee, in charge of building construction.

PHILLIPE a pilot among Basil's Bastards who was drowned in a glacial stream at the foot of Monte Rosa.

PHOBOSUCHUS (foh-boh-SOO-kus) also called "Deinosuchus," an enormous crocodilian up to 15 meters in length, whose fossils are found in Upper Cretaceous strata of Europe and North America. We fancifully allow it to persist into the Pliocene as a predator of the plesiosaur.

PHYLLIS-MORIGEL name assumed by Felice while disguised as a gold-torc on the way to Muriah. *See also* Morigel.

PIMPLE KNOB a small eminence on the north side of Monte Rosa.

PINGOL THE HORRIPILANT (PIN-g'l) bushy-haired Firvulag, leader of a troop of stalwart gnomes.

PITKIN, CASTELLAN silver-torc human administrator of Castle Gateway.

PK *See* Psychokinesis.

PLAIN OF SPORTS a section of Muriah containing racecourses and a small arena.

PLAQUE-BOOK an audiovisual device of the Milieu, typically about the size of a twentieth-century paperback book. The plaque had a liquid-crystal display in color or black and white and could be programmed with the contents of any book by inserting it into a library machine and paying the fee. Pressing one of the four corners of the plaque "turned the pages" slowly or rapidly, forward or reverse. Plaques could be reprogrammed or stored with the contents intact virtually indefinitely. Larger format plaques were used for picture books, maps, graphs, and the like. Paged books were not entirely obsolete in the Milieu, but they were expensive compared to the plaques.

PLASS slang term for plastic, in general use by the time of the Intervention.

PLESIOSAUR a large marine reptile of the suborder Plesiosauria, *not* a dinosaur. Plesiosaurs had long necks, small heads, paddle-shaped limbs, and ovoid or spindle-shaped bodies with a long tail. The true Plesiosauridae seem to have become extinct by the end of the Jurassic; but similar animals of the related Elasmosauridae are found in Upper Cretaceous strata. It has been speculated that the Loch Ness Monster represents a relict landlocked population of plesiosaurs. We fancifully place the creature in the Lower Pliocene, together with Phobosuchus as its predator.

PLIKTHARN (PLIK-th'ah'rn)   dwarf scout and courier at the Finiah invasion.

PLIKTOL (PLIK-tawl)   name given to a river of the Hercynian Forest, a tributary of the Nonol, analogous to the Proto-Armançon. Its name means "Green River."

PLIOCENE EPOCH (PLY-uh-seen)   that part of the Cenozoic Era preceding the Pleistocene (PLY-stuh-seen) Ice Ages. It has long been an orphan of indistinct boundaries among geologists, since its divisions are not readily separable from those of the Upper Miocene. I have followed Milieu practice by beginning the Pliocene Epoch with the rise of the Hipparion Fauna of "Pontain" times—some 10–11 million years B.P. This would be the Late Tortonian of some authorities, the Vallesian of others. I would end the Pliocene about 3 million years B.P., at the first onset of continental glaciation.

POLCHRO (PAH'l-kroh)   an iridescent luxury fabric of the Milieu, resembling moiré satin.

POLITY   any of the six great racial "communities" of the Galactic Milieu. Lylmik, Krondak, Gi, Poltroyan, Simbiari, and Human Polities are autonomous in ordinary government matters, but supervised by the Concilium, which has representatives from each polity. *See also* Galactic Milieu.

POLTROY, AMALGAM OF   the Poltroyan Polity of the Galactic Milieu, including those planets colonized by the small, red-eyed people so similar to humanity in superficial appearance and so unlike them in physiology. The Poltroyans are famed for their urbane diplomatism, which blunter races deem facile. They tend to view life as a cosmic joke that should be savored to the fullest, and with this end in view were early supporters of the Lylmik, favoring the Intervention. Poltroyans are very numerous in the Milieu and have a thriving trade and social intercourse with the Human Polity.

POROFILM   a material used for dressing open wounds.

POSTDILUVIUM   the time in the Many-Colored Land following the Flood, especially the months before Aiken-Lugonn assumed the Tanu throne.

PRENTICE BROWN, GREGORY   *See* Greg-Donnet.

PRISCHCHEPA   a Cossack time-traveler killed while trying to escape from Castle Gateway.

PROGAN   a Milieu medication that speeds healing.

PROLEPSIS   also called prescience, precognition, foresight, or "the sight," it is a metafaculty that includes prediction or visualization of future events, apparently through some psychic manipulation of the temporal lattices. The faculty is rare and virtually uncontrollable among humans. The Lylmik are alleged to have significant proleptic talents; but since they decline to submit to analysis, their power can only be studied indirectly through their actions. Brede Shipspouse displayed proleptic talent in carrying the Tanu and Firvulag to Earth, and in her unclear vision of Elizabeth's role in exotic-human destiny. Mayvar Kingmaker and Morna-Ia, also, were proleptic.

PROMEPHITIS (proh-meh-FY-tih's)   a small skunklike animal widespread in the European Pliocene.

PROTO-ANDARAX (AHN-dah-rah'sh)   name given to a Spanish Pliocene river draining south from Mount Mulhacén into the Great Brackish Marsh.

PROTO-AUGUSTA   a Pliocene river of northern Italy, analogous to the modern Aosta.

PROTO-JÚCAR (HOO-kah'r)   a Pliocene river of southern Koneyn analogous to the modern watercourse. Afaliah lay near its mouth. It emptied into the Catalan Gulf.

PROTO-RHINE   a principal European watercourse during the Pliocene. In its upper reaches it maintained a course similar to that of the modern river. But farther north on the continent its course wandered. Eventually it merged with the Proto-Thames and the combined stream poured into the Anversian Sea, an arm of the Atlantic, forming a great delta.

PROVENÇAL, LAC (proh-vah'ng-SAH'l, lah'k)   name given to the sheet of shallow water and everglade at the mouth of the Pliocene Rhône. This lake is one of the author's more speculative features. Following the refilling of the Mediterranean, this region became an embayment of the sea, with the Rhône Valley flooded north almost to Lyon.

PSEUDAILURUS (sood-ay-LOO-rus)   a primitive felid about the size of a lynx, common in Pliocene Europe.

PSYCHOCREATIVE BUBBLE or SCREEN   a shield of mental energy, usually transparent, more or less impervious to matter and to energy below the visual spectrum. Stalwart Tanu creators and Firvulag routinely generated small psychocreative screens to shield themselves. Massed metaconcerted screens were not common among either nation until the Postdiluvium.

PSYCHOKINESIS or PK   one of the primary meta-faculties, involving the ability of a mind to move or otherwise manipulate matter. Levitation is an aspect of PK. In pre-Intervention days, so-called poltergeist phenomena were a product of mostly subconscious PK on the part of disturbed persons, especially youths. The Milieu regarded PK as the least valuable metafunction, although PK adepts were valued in micromanipulation and in certain delicate healing operations. Milieu operants possessing a high PK function were more likely to conceal the fact than glory in it. Among the Tanu, it was a valued aspect of the armamentarium, used not only in aggression but also combined with redaction in the Skin healing process. An old name for PK is telekinesis.

PSYCHOKINETIC GUILD   one of the five great Guilds Mental of the Tanu. In the earliest days of the Tanu sojourn on Earth it was headed by Minanonn the Proud, Battlemaster of the Threefold Function. After he was declared heretic, Nodonn headed the guild, with the twins Kuhal Earthshaker and Fian Skybreaker as joint Second. King Aiken-Lugonn undertook the guild presidency upon his ascent to the throne. (He was also Lord Coercer and Lord Creator.) His deputy was Bleyn the Champion, and his on-again, off-again Second was Kuhal Earthshaker. The heraldic colors of the psychokinetics were rose-gold (halide pink) and gold.

PSYCHOZAP   a blast of psychocreative energy used aggressively. Its ultimate source was the chemical decomposition of water or atmospheric molecules.

PURTSINIGELEE SPECKLEBELLY (PURT-suh-NIG-uh-lee) Firvulag resident on Monte Rosa, a harvester of giant slugs.

PUSHFACE nom d'exil of one of Basil's Bastards, a technician.

QUEST among the Tanu, a large-scale Hunt mounted as a punitive expedition, or for some other extraordinary motive.

QUICKSILVER CAVE a disused Firvulag mercury mine, near the junction of the Great South Road and the Amalizan Track, the scene of Aiken's mental rebirth.

QUIGLEY, SUNNY JIM a young third-generation Lowlife, originally a denizen of the Paris Basin swamp. He emerged to seek his fortune after the Flood, joined forces with Vilkas, and became an ashigaru, or man-at-arms, attending Yosh Watanabe.

RAIMO   *See* Hakkinen, Raimo.

RAMAPITHECUS or RAMA (rah-mah-PIH-thee-kus)   a genus of small hominid ape, apparently widespread in the Late Miocene and Early Pliocene of Asia and Europe. The first fossils were from India. Much confusion has resulted from a multiplicity of generic names being assigned to what is probably a single hominid genus. The matter is complicated by the fragmentary nature of the fossil remains. Ramapithecus was about the size of a five- or six-year-old European child. It stood upright and had a remarkable vertical face. After years of controversy, it has finally been widely acknowledged that it belongs on the direct hominid line, pushing human roots back some 15 million years B.P. As already noted in the first Appendix to *The Golden Torc*, I place Ramapithecus as late as the Pontian by virtue of "Graecopithecus freybergi" of von Koenigswald, reinforced by material assembled by Kurtén. The ape is thought to have been a forest-dweller.

REAM   a brutal redactive technique used to extract information from a subject's memory. A particularly damaging type is called deep-ream.

REBELLION, METAPSYCHIC   an uprising of human metapsychics against the Milieu, climaxing in 2083. The ostensible motive for the conflict was the refusal of the five exotic races to approve the Mental Man project for accelerated human evolution, championed by Marc Remillard and his faction. Deeper than that was the fear, among "normal" humans as well as metas, that Unity (the ultimate symbiosis of the human World Mind with the Mind of the Galaxy) would somehow deprive humans of their individual personalities and free will. There was also the well-known fact that the human race had a far greater potential than the exotics for both population growth and metapsychic growth; human chauvinists suspected that the exotics would use Unity to put limits on humanity. Humans loyal to the Milieu were led by Marc's brother Jon and Jon's wife, Dorothea Macdonald, or Diamond Mask. The Rebel faction was provoked to violence only during the last months of the affair, when what had been an intellectual debate turned into a war threatening to destroy the Milieu. The history of the Rebellion is detailed in the Milieu Trilogy.

REDACTION (ree-DAK-shun)   also called psychic healing, mind-alteration, or mental editing, the rarest of the primary metapsychic faculties, involving the ability of a mind to exert healing power upon its own body or mind or the body or mind of another. The qualities of empathy and solace also belong to this function. Misuse of the function is exemplified in so-called mind-reaming, and various kinds of mental torture.

REDACTOR GUILD   the smallest of the five great Guilds Mental of the Tanu. Before the Flood, its president was

Dionket Lord Healer. His Second was Culluket the Interrogator, a combatant redactor. Most members of the guild were mental healers, not fighters. The secret Peace Faction included many redactors. Many members of the guild survived the Flood because they were attending Combat casualties in Redactor House, high above Muriah. These later participated in the exodus from Aven and accompanied Dionket to Minanonn's enclave in the Pyrénées. The first Lord Redactor under Aiken-Lugonn was Culluket, who had no Second. After his death, Boduragol was named President and his wife Credela was Second. The heraldic colors of the guild are ruby-red and white or silver.

REDON, STRAIT OF (reh-DOH'ng) during the Pliocene, a channel of the Atlantic Ocean separating Breton Island from the mainland of Armorica.

REGEN-TANK Milieu slang for regeneration-tank, a device used for repairing human physical trauma or for rejuvenation (q.v.). It utilized the patient's own redactive forces as well as artificial healing impulses and was capable of restoring almost any kind of injury or degeneration, provided life was not completely extinct in the subject. The technique of regeneration improved steadily throughout the twenty-first century. The equipment brought to the Pliocene by the ex-Rebels was already "primitive" by the time the Saga opens. *See also* Skin.

REJUVENATION a form of regeneration-tank therapy that tended to reverse the human aging process. It utilized the implanation of fresh genetic material as well as the repair of broken-down tissues. The rejuvenation process was rarely carried out to the point of unseemly youthfulness. Most middle-aged or elderly rejuvenates preferred a reasonably mature appearance consonant with their mental outlook, and were restored to an apparent age of thirty-five to forty-five. As technology improved, this rejuvenated appearance was sustained for a longer and longer period. By 2110, some people had undergone four rejuvenative courses, and there seemed no reason why they might not live indefinitely if they wanted to.

REMILLARD (REM-ih-lard) their own pronunciation in Standard English—the most prominent family of human metapsychics. See "The Remillard Family Tree" in this *Pliocene Companion*. The Remillards anciently originated in Québec Province, Canada, and migrated to the U.S. in the middle nineteenth century. The patriarch of the metapsychic clan and genetic founder of the "immortality" strain was Donatien (Don) Remillard, born 1945 in the mill town of Berlin, N.H. Don's son Denis, the noted metapsychologist, fathered the main line. The history of the Remillards is told in the Milieu Trilogy.

REMILLARD, CLOUD born 2082, daughter and second child of Marc Remillard and Cyndia Muldowney, taken to the Pliocene as an infant by her father.

REMILLARD, DENIS born 1967, eldest child of Don, became Chairman of the Department of Metapsychology at Darmouth College, N.H., in 2009. He married his colleague, Lucille Cartier, in 1995 and they had seven operant children. The youngest and most powerful was Paul. Denis and Lucille and their associates were responsible for the Great Intervention (q.v.).

REMILLARD, [DENIS] HAGEN (HAH-g'n) born 2080, elder child of Marc Remillard and Cyndia Muldowney, taken to the Pliocene as a small child by his father. Although christened Denis, he was always called Hagen, a name his mother insisted on bestowing for symbolic reasons.

REMILLARD, JON, called JACK THE BODILESS born 2052, the youngest child of Paul Remillard and Teresa

Kendall, the brother of Marc and husband of Dorothea Macdonald, called Diamond Mask. He possessed all five metafunctions at a Paramount Grand Master level and was also the greatest metaconcert designer of his time. From his mother he inherited the sublethal "bodiless" mutagene. His history is detailed in the Milieu Trilogy.

REMILLARD, LUC born 2041, fifth child of Paul Remillard and Teresa Kendall.

REMILLARD, MADELEINE born 2040, fourth child of Paul Remillard and Teresa Kendall.

REMILLARD, MARC born 2038, oldest child of Paul Remillard and Teresa Kendall. He became a Paramount Grand Master farsensor, coercer, and creator, and was a magnate of the Concilium. Marc was the second greatest metaconcert designer in the Milieu, surpassed only by his brother Jon. He married Cyndia Muldowney in 2080. Marc's scheme for accelerating human evolution, called Mental Man, was a basic cause of the Metapsychic Rebellion. At first a respected leader, he later gained a fearsome reputation when he led a force in a direct confrontation with the Milieu. He was called the Angel of the Abyss, the Destroyer, and Abaddon because of his brilliance, his commanding aspect, and his pride. His history is told in the Milieu Trilogy and in the last two books of the Saga. Marc was actually a fraternal twin; his brother Matthieu died shortly after birth.

REMILLARD, MARIE born 2039, third child of Paul Remillard and Teresa Kendall.

REMILLARD, MATTHIEU born 2038, fraternal twin brother to Marc, he died shortly after birth.

REMILLARD, PAUL, called "THE MAN WHO SOLD NEW HAMPSHIRE" born 2014, youngest child of Denis

Remillard and Lucille Cartier and the only one of their offspring to receive Milieu-style mental training in utero. He became the first human magnate of the Concilium and played a pivotal role in the formation of the Human Polity. Paul was a consummate politician and a powerful meta-psychic. In 2037 he married Teresa Kendall. Five of their children, all operant, survived to adulthood. The oldest was Marc and the youngest Jon. Paul's history is detailed in the Milieu Trilogy.

RENIAN GLASSCRAFTER (RAY-nee-un)   a top-ranking member of the Creator Guild at Muriah.

REPELVEL   a water-repellent velvet fabric of the Milieu.

RHO-FIELD   one of the primary aspects of reality, a dynamic field utilized in "inertialess" gravo-magnetically powered aircraft and subluminal spacecraft. The rho-field is most commonly manifest in a network of crawling purplish light clothing the skin of a vehicle powered by a rho-activated flux-tapper. The web has a powerful (lethal to humans) electrical component that is usually shielded by a force-screen in Milieu vehicles. The rhocraft of the Duat exotics utilized a naked web.

RICHARD   *See* Voorhees, Richard.

RICHTER, KARL JOSEF   a German poet who became the first human time-traveler to the Pliocene. He was translated by Madame Guderian in 2041.

RIES (reez)   *See* Ship's Grave.

RIF MOUNTAINS   a range in northwestern Africa. During the Pliocene it joined a low range across Gibraltar, this connecting with the Betics to form a sharply bent arc around the western end of the Mediterranean Basin.

RIGANONE (rih-GAH-noh'n)   a member of King Thagdal's High Table, a stalwart of the Host, Second Farsensor under Mayvar. She was killed in the Last Grand Combat.

RING-HOCKEY   a violent sport of the planet Acadie, played by Felice. Team members mounted on large animals called verruls attempted to move a plastic ring into a goal-hopper, at the same time avoiding stun-gun attacks by the opposition.

RIVIERA   a cosmop planet in the Human Polity, much esteemed by vacationers.

ROCCARO, ANNAMARIA, called SISTER AMERIE   Roman Catholic priest and physician, a member of Group Green. She was thirty-seven years old when she went to the Pliocene, wishing to become a hermit. She became active in the Lowlife freedom movement and joined the attack of the Muriah torc works. After the Flood she was a close associate of Elizabeth on the exodus from Aven. When Elizabeth retired to Black Crag, Amerie went to Hidden Springs with Chief Burke. On the way she met Brother Anatoly and persuaded him to become Elizabeth's spiritual counselor.

ROCILAN (ROH-sih-lah'n)   nicknamed Candy City, a Tanu city on the Gulf of Aquitaine, north of the Bordeaux Estuary. Its City-Lord at the time of the Last Grand Combat was Gradlonn. After the Flood, Gradlonn's widow Eadnar married Alberonn and the two of them ruled jointly. Rocilan was surrounded by sugar plantations and coconut and cacao groves. Fruits, nuts, and other raw materials for confectionary processing were shipped to it from the farms along the River Baar. In addition to candy, Rocilan produced liqueurs, brandies, and wines. It also had a small pearl fishery, manned by humans. The modern Île de Ré marks the approximate site of Rocilan.

RONIAH (roh-NY-uh)   Tanu city situated on the west bank of the Rhône River, in the approximate location of modern Lyon. The name means "Fast (River) City." The original exotic name for the river, Ronaar ("Fast River"), was abbreviated with the coming of humanity. Roniah was a transportation center surrounded by plantations and regions rich in wild game. An annual Fair was held there during the Pre-Combat Truce. Prior to the Flood, Roniah was ruled by Bormol. Condateyr Fulminator became City-Lord in the Postdiluvium.

RONIN (roh-nih'n)   in Japanese, a masterless samurai, a "wave man" adrift on the sea of life. In old Japan, ronin might find themselves unattached for a number of reasons: the master might have suffered political disaster; the master might have fired the knight for some offense—either serious or petty; or the master might have perished in battle. Ronin tried to earn a living by teaching bujutsu, by becoming bodyguards or mercenaries, or by resorting to banditry. They had a romantic and ferocious image, retaining their honor. Sometimes they combined in large numbers so as to become a serious threat to weaker feudal lords.

ROOM WITHOUT DOORS   a gravo-magnetically powered force-field with self-contained life support, impervious to entering matter, energy, and mental energy, but transparent to the same exiting. It can be programmed to admit only a single individual. Those inside it are always free to exit. It is virtually indestructible and impenetrable, a product of ancient Duat Galaxy technology unequalled by any Milieu device.

ROSA, MONTE   in the Pliocene Exile, the highest mountain in the world, with an elevation of 9082 meters. This designation is boldly made by the author by virtue of the alleged supereminence of the Monte Rosa Nappe, the crest of the Pennine Alps, which during the Pliocene thrust toward the Po Basin like some petrified tsunami. In Milieu times Rosa was the second highest peak in Europe (after Mont Blanc), at 4634 meters. It was planed down by the Ice Ages and probably downwarped as well. The massif is still awesome, crowned by glaciers, but not a particularly difficult climb. It is easily reached from a base in Zermatt.

ROSMAR (roh'z-MAH'r) *See* Lamballe, Mercedes.

ROWANE (roh-AY'n) Howler woman of Nionel, who became Tony Wayland's wife.

RUAN, YOBBO human gold miner of Amalizan, later at the Fennoscandian diggings.

RUBBERBAND EFFECT or WITHDRAWAL HYPER-SNAP a phenomenon of hyperspatial translation, whereby the traveling object tends to be pulled back to its point of origin—either as it emerges from the terminal u-field or even "after" it has apparently exited safely at its destination. The effect is believed to result from imperfect meshing of the spatio-temporal lattices.

RUTH, SISTER a Catholic priest resident in Goriah.

RYFA THE INSATIABLE (RY-fuh) a "wild" Firvulag ogress in the Maritime Alps.

SAASTAMOINEN, VEIKKO (SAH-stuh-moy-n'n, VY-koh) a member of Ocala's second generation, the son of Walter Saastamoinen and Solange Forester. He was a talented farsensor and the mate of Irena O'Malley.

SAASTAMOINEN, WALTER ex-Rebel of Ocala, once Deputy Chief Starfleet Operations (Strategy) under Ragnar Gathen. He built the great schooner Kyllikki and was her master. He was the husband of Solange Forester and the father of Veikko.

SALIM one of the guardians at Castle Gateway at the time of Group Green's arrival.

SALOTE (sah-LOH-tay) female silver-torc Polynesian attendant at the Calamosk baths.

SANCHEZ, MARIPOSA DE famed pizza restauranteur captured by Firvulag.

SANDERS a scientist of Londinium, who visited Théophile Guderian shortly before the professor's death.

SANDRA   a Lowlife woman of Hidden Springs, cured by Sister Amerie.

SANDVIK, BENGT   pilot among Basil's Bastards who participated in the final assault on Monte Rosa.

SAYZORASK (SAY-zoh-rah'sk)   a small Tanu town on the northern shore of Lac Provençal, near the debouchment of the Rhône. Its City-Lord was Lomnovel, who survived the Flood and became a member of Aiken's High Table. Its name means "Fort Resolute." Sayzorask was an important caravan stop on the Great South Road.

SCHWARZWALD   *See* Black Forest.

SEABORG, COMMANDER   gold-torc human garrison commander at Finiah who was slain during the invasion.

SEBI-GOMNOL   *See* Gomnol.

SEEKERSENSE   an aspect of farsensing that can be programmed to home in on some mental signature or clearly visualized object.

SEEKOL (SEE-kawl)   Firvulag name given to the lower reaches of the Pliocene Seine. It means "Deep River."

SENDING   *See* Simulacrum.

SENIET LORD HISTORIAN (seh-n'YET)   a worthy of the Creator Guild, present at Mercy's first challenge of Aluteyn.

SEUNG KYU   a gray-torc soldier escorting Creyn's party to Roniah.

SHAPE-SHIFTING   an aspect of creativity, usually involving the projection of an illusion that changes one's appearance. Some higher forms of shape-shifting involve actual manipulation of the molecules and real physical change. The Firvulag illusions were simple mental projections.

SHARN-ADOR (shah'rn uh-DOH'r)   eldest son of King Sharn-Mes and Queen Ayfa; his baby name was Smudger. His illusory aspect was that of a wart-biter locust.

SHARN-MES, called SHARN THE YOUNGER (shah'rn-MES)   at the time of Group Green's arrival in the Pliocene, a Great Captain and battlehero of the Firvulag, deputy to Pallol Battlemaster, who during Pallol's default led the Firvulag forces in the Grand Combat. His wife was Ayfa and they had six children, the eldest Sharn-Ador, all under seven years of age. Sharn was shrewd and open to innovation, four generations removed from the First Comers of his race. After the Flood, the Gnomish Council unanimously elected him and Ayfa co-monarchs. Expediency, not tradition, moved Sharn to instigate Nightfall, which he and Ayfa saw as an opportunity to finish off the Tanu once and for all.

SHARN THE ATROCIOUS (Sharn Octriol)   great-great-grandfather of Sharn-Mes, First Comer Firvulag battlemaster, who fought the Great Ordeal at the Ship's Grave with Bright Lugonn and was defeated. The Sword of Sharn is named in his honor.

SHAUNAVON, CLAIRE   ex-Rebel at Ocala, mother of Matiwilda Shaunavon.

SHAUNAVON, MATIWILDA   a member of Ocala's second generation, daughter of Claire Shaunavon, a self-taught physicist.

SHERWOODE, ALLISON   an ex-Rebel at Ocala, former Communications Coordinator of the Rebel armada and farsensor, badly brain-burned during the Rebellion. She was the mother of André Sherwoode-Laroche.

SHINTY   the Tanu name for the game of hurley (q.v.).

SHIP   a gigantic crystalline organism, sapient and metafunctional, an inhabitant of interstellar space in the Duat Galaxy. Ships were capable of superluminal travel through mental generation of an upsilon-field. They were entirely benevolent and many of them undertook a symbiotic "mind-marriage" with humanoid females of the Duat daughter-worlds. Ships routinely carried the Duat citizenry on intragalactic voyages of great distance, the passengers traveling within a vessel embedded in the Ship's crystal body. A mitigator program transmitted by the Ship to its passengers enabled humanoids to go superluminal without pain. Ships also executed very tight subspace catenaries, attaining their destinations much faster than the mechanical starships used by Duat peoples for shortdistance transport.

SHIP'S GRAVE   name given to the Ries or Rieskessel, a huge meteoric crater now surrounding the German city of Nördlingen north of the Danube. It is discussed in the first Appendix to *The Golden Torc*. In the saga, the crater marks the impact point where the crystalline corpse of Brede's Ship fell to Earth. Following a commemorative Great Ordeal (q.v.), Tanu and Firvulag First Comers left their orbiter aircraft parked around the rim of the crater lake. The locale of the Ship's Grave was expunged from the racial memory.

SHIPSPOUSE   *See* Brede Shipspouse.

SHONKWILER, COUNSELOR   functionary at l'Auberge du Portail, upon whom Felice wreaked mayhem.

SHOPILTEE BLOODGUZZLER (SHOH-pih'l-tee)   a dwarf Firvulag stalwart at the Grand Tourney.

SHQIPNI (sh'KEEP-nee)   an "Albanian" planet of the Human Polity.

SHUBASH   gray-torc guardian at Castle Gateway when Group Green arrived.

SIBEL LONGTRESS (sih-BEL)   female farsensor Tanu, named by Aiken to his High Table as Second under Morna-Ia. She was an old flame of Minanonn's.

SIGMA-FIELD   one of the primary aspects of reality, a dynamic field intimately bound into the spatial dimensions of "normal" space-time. In its purer manifestation it was utilized in the generation of forceshields, screens, and barricades. It also has psychocreative analogs. The term sigma-field, or sigma, is commonly applied to the shield phenomenon itself, which looks from the "outside" like a silvery mirror and from the "inside" like a more-or-less transparent interface. Sigma force-fields vary greatly in impermeability, according to the type of generator used. Personal screens designed to protect one against psycho-creative aggression or the commoner Milieu weapons are semipermeable pseudospatial membranes allowing atmospheric gases up to and including atomic number 10 (neon) free transfer. Thus one can breathe inside them. The more powerful screens, such as the great SR-35 and the SR-15, are virtually impermeable and require a self-contained atmosphere. Sigmas can be farsensed through dimly at close range only. Certain weapons can be phased to fire through them from "inside" without disrupting the field. Touching a sigma-field is not hazardous.

SIGMUND   Lowlife who accompanied Khalid Khan on the first iron-seeking expedition.

SIMBIARI, pl., **SIMB**, sing. (sih'm-bee-AH-ree)   one of the coadunate exotic races of the Milieu, the youngest but for humanity. The Simbiari, though keenly intelligent and noted scientists, are bumptious clods entirely lacking in social grace. Their physiology is peculiarly repellent to humans. Of amphibian stock, the Simbiari skin is coated with a slimy green mucus that tends to drip off, especially when the Simb is excited or stressed. The Simbiari are notorious for crude practical jokes and tactless behavior. It is thought that their surveillance crews were responsible for most of the malevolent "flying saucer" encounters during pre-Intervention days.

SIMULACRUM   a psychocreative apparition, usually of the body of the originator, varying in substantiality according to the mental skill of the generator. It can be projected across a distance. Tanu and Firvulag call such a manifestation a "sending." When Marc Remillard appeared to interpenetrate the armor of his CE rig, he was actually generating a simulacrum.

SINGER-DOW, FRIEDA   ex-Rebel of Ocala, wife of Lu-Shen Chan and mother of Chee-Wu Chan.

SINGING STONE   a new trophy crafted by the Firvulag for the Grand Tourney, when it was believed that both the Sword and the Spear had been lost in the Flood. It was an enormous beryl, carved in the shape of a regal field stool and programmed to play a phrase of sonorous music when sat upon by the true High King of the Many-Colored Land. It was to be programmed to the victorious monarch's aura, and any lesser person who ventured to sit upon it would die. It has an interesting parallel in the Lia Fail of Irish legend and the Stone of Scone sacred to the Scots. The melody it sings is identical to the Rhine River leitmotiv in Wagner's *Ring* cycle (symbolizing the river as "undifferentiated nature," according to Donington).

SKATHE THE DREADFUL (s'KAY'th)   a Great Captain of the Fighting Ogresses and close friend of Ayfa. She was a member of the Gnomish Council.

SKIN   a psychoactive substance resembling transparent plastic, used by the Tanu to wrap sick or injured persons prior to their being subjected to mental healing. The Skin was a highly sophisticated variant of the regen-tank that "aimed" redactive and psychokinetic impulses of the healer at appropriate parts of the body within, while screening out other psychic emanations that might impair recovery. The patient's own redaction was also enhanced by Skin.

SLITSAL (SLIH't-sah'l)   a Firvulag exclamation meaning "hail!" or "good health!" equivalent of the Tanu slon-shal; it was delivered vivace as an accolade. Cf. YLAHAYLL.

SLONSHAL (SLAH'n-sh'l)   Tanu exclamation meaning "hail!" or "good health!" equivalent of the Firvulag slitsal. It is eerily evocative of the Gaelic "Slainte."

SMOKEY   Lowlife of Hidden Springs who accompanied Khalid Khan's iron-seeking expedition.

SMUDGER   *See* Sharn-Ador.

SMUTS, EVA   ex-Rebel of Ocala, mate to Nanomea Fox and co-mother of Kané Fox-Laroche.

SNEETCH   in Milieu slang, a patching up of some bungled job or assignment, especially when the attempt at rectification is incompetent.

SONG, THE   the great anthem of both Tanu and Firvulag, sung at many solemn occasions and also at the beginning of day (sunrise). It was used as a welcome, as a funeral hymn, at the Grand Loving, the Grand Combat, and the Grand Tourney. Its imagery harks back to Duat.

The third verse was only to be sung at Nightfall. The melody of the Tanu Song is given in the second Appendix to *The Many-Colored Land*. It has close affinities to "Londonderry Air," a tune traditionally attributed to Gaelic faerie folk. The Firvulag version of the song was more complex, designed to produce a striking polyphonic effect, a grand exotic motet, when the Songs of both races were sung together.

SONIC DISRUPTOR a Milieu weapon using ultrasound impulses to lacerate or dissolve flesh.

SOUTHERN LAGOONS before the Flood, name given to bodies of salt water in the Mediterranean Basin south of the Aven Peninsula. They were connected by shallow channels.

SPACE, NORMAL in the New Universal Field Theory, the phenomenon generated by the spatio-temporal lattices, upon whose nodes matter and energy interface with time and mind. It is contrasted with hyperspace (q.v.) and mental space—the latter generated by the fundamental matrix lattices (alpha, beta, and gamma) and sometimes called "realm of spirit." *See also* Lattice; Dynamic Field.

SPEAR OF LUGONN a powerful photonic weapon in the shape of a jousting lance, originally made for the battlemaster Bright Lugonn in the Duat Galaxy. The Spear, in Duat legend, was the principal Tanu weapon in the Nightfall War. Its lowest power-setting was used in ritual combat between battlemasters. The higher settings were for use against "extraordinary obstacles to the racial destiny." In practice, the photon cannon setting served to fend off opposition forces of the Duat daughter-worlds when they pursued the remnant of Tanu and Firvulag to Void's Edge. *See also* Sword of Sharn.

STANDARD ENGLISH *See* English, Standard.

STAR OF MORNING *See* Adversary.

STEFANKO (steh-FAH'n-koh) Lowlife of Hidden Springs, a laser technician, killed by a giant pig on the first Ship's Grave Expedition. He was a special friend of Martha.

STEIN *See* Oleson, Stein.

STEINBRENNER, JEFFREY ex-Rebel at Ocala, formerly director of Marc Remillard's Mental Man laboratories. He was a magnate of the Concilium, a physician, embryologist, and genetic engineer.

STEM-SHIELD a mental or mechanical defense of the brain stem, most vulnerable part of that organ.

STENDAL a silver-torc associate of Tony Wayland in Finiah prior to its invasion.

STILL-VEXED BERMOOTHES name given by whimsical ex-Rebels of Ocala Island to a chain of coral islets lying southeast of their home. (Cf. *The Tempest*, Act I, Sc. 2, 229.) *See also* the maps of Ocala in this *Pliocene Companion*.

STIM-VIM a vitamin-laced stimulant drug favored by athletes and laborers in the Milieu.

STRANGFORD, CHRIS (Christopher) a member of Ocala's second generation, son of Helayne Strangford. He was the mate of Leila Jacoby. Their son was Joel.

STRANGFORD, HELAYNE ex-Rebel of Ocala, former magnate of the Concilium and a metaconcert expert who had been one of the most powerful coercers among Marc's supporters. She was seriously deranged after the failure of the Rebellion.

STRANGFORD, JOEL a member of Ocala's third generation, the four-and-one-half-year-old son of Chris Strangford and Leila Jacoby.

STUN-GUN a common Milieu weapon, such as the Husqvarna Mk VI-G. If its electromagnetic beam strikes the brain or spinal cord of a target organism, instant unconsciousness results, usually without lasting harmful effect. The stun-charge of the "Husky" weapons commonly smuggled into the Pliocene was adjustable; the target could be stunned only momentarily or knocked out for up to two days.

SUBLUMINAL adjective meaning "slower than light," referring to spacecraft traveling through normal space, as opposed to hyperspatial translation. Subluminal flight was used in the vicinity of tenanted planetary systems and for short hops. Most subluminal propulsion systems utilized the "inertialess drive" of the rho-field.

SUBSPACE COMMUNICATION communication within the hyperspatial matrix. A special unit invented by the Krondaku enabled ships traveling in the gray limbo to communicate with each other, provided their catenaries were not too incongruent. It was not possible for these ships to communicate with sources outside hyperspace. Subject to certain limitations, farsened communication was also possible in hyperspace—but not between hyperspace and normal space.

SUBSUMPTION, METAPSYCHIC a rare phenomenon whereby the primary metafunctions of one person are completely assimilated by another: the ultimate in brain-draining. It inevitably causes the death of the drainee and could also be fatal to the drainer. Only the Poltroyans, among Milieu peoples, had any reliable experience with subsumptions. *See also* Metapsychic Complexus.

SUGOLL (SOO-goh'l) the leader of the Meadow Mountain Howlers, eventually made Prince of that nation under Sharn and Ayfa. He exceeded all his mutant subjects in physical abomination, but usually wore a handsome illusory body. He married Katlinel the Dark-eyed, a Tanu-human hybrid, and ruled the city of Nionel.

SUKEY *See* Davies, Sue-Gwen.

SULLIVAN-TONN (tah'n) Tanu sobriquet given to Aloysius X. Sullivan, in the Milieu a professor of moral theology at Fordham University. A powerful latent psychokinetic, he was granted a gold torc and became a loyal assistant to Velteyn of Finiah. He helped evacuate the doomed city and later went to Calamosk, where his teenaged fiancée Olone was trying vainly to rule after her parents had perished in the Flood. Sullivan lasted only a few months there before being driven out by Aluteyn. He and Olone took refuge with Aiken in Goriah. He was jealous of Aiken because of his young wife's infatuation with the Nonborn King.

SUNNY JIM *See* Quigley, Sunny Jim.

SUPERFICIES in the New Universal Field Theory, the boundary or surface of any three- to six-dimensional phenomenon. The term is used in common parlance for the upsilon-field "gateway" between normal space and hyperspace, for a time-gate, and for the boundary of a sigma-field screen.

SUPERLUMINAL adjective meaning "faster than light," referring to spacecraft traveling through hyperspace, as opposed to normal-space locomotion. Superluminal travel is discussed in the fourth Appendix to *The Adversary*. The term was in general use late in the twentieth century.

SWABIAN ALB a low mountain range extending in a northeasterly direction from the Black Forest; the Schwäbische Alb. In the Pliocene, a region inhabited by Howlers.

SWORD OF SHARN a powerful photonic weapon in the shape of a great two-handed sword, made for the Battlemaster Sharn the Atrocious in the Duat Galaxy. In Duat legend, the Sword would be used by the Firvulag during the Nightfall War fought against the Tanu Foe. Its lowest setting was for ritual fighting in the Encounter of Battlemasters, and the higher ones were for defending the nation against "extraordinary menaces"—e.g., the vessels of the Duat Federation that hounded the battle-religion recalcitrants to Void's Edge. Later, the Sword became the Grand Combat trophy and was only used ritually in the Opening of the Sky.

SYNCHRONICITY a word coined by C. G. Jung, "an acausal connecting principle" or generator of "meaningful coincidences." In lectures he equated it with Tao. In metapsychology, it has proleptic and creative aspects. *See also* Metafunction.

SYNCHRONOUS TIME a tau-lattice effect linking Pliocene time with Milieu time, thus making the Guderian time-portal feasible. It should *not* be confused with synchronicity. For an indeterminate number of years prior to and following the opening and closing of the portal, Earth's rotation and orbital revolution during the Pliocene and during the later Milieu epoch were precisely synchronized; i.e., the respective times coincided so that noon on the Lyon meridian in the Milieu coincided with noon at Castle Gateway some 6 million years earlier on the same date.

SYNERGY, MENTAL joint mental action, as in metaconcert; not to be confused with Unity. In synergy, the total output exceeds the sum of the input.

TAGAN LORD OF SWORDS (tuh-GAH'n) a great Tanu hero and fighting specialist, responsible for training human gladiators for the Grand Combat. Like many warrior types, he belonged to the Coercer Guild. Tagan sat on the High Table.

TAINTED SWAMP a wetland near the mouth of the Laar River, a breeding place for plesiosaurs and a haunt of giant crocodiles.

TALLAHATCHIE an "American" planet of the Human Polity, former residence of Skipper Highjohn.

TAMIAMI an "American" planet in the Human Polity.

TAMLIN THE MEPHITIC (TAM-lih'n) a Firvulag musk oil processor of the Monte Rosa region.

TANA (TAH-nuh) *See* Goddess.

TANU (TAH-noo) or People of the Goddess, the tall, slender, generally fair-haired and fair-skinned nation of the dimorphous Duat race, probably the most primitive of the Duat humanoid stock. They were engendered in the equatorial regions of the mother planet, lands perennially clouded, hot, and humid. Their sensitive eyes showed pinpoint pupils in the bright sunlight of Pliocene Earth. The Tanu were metapsychic latents who long ago had developed the psychic amplifier called the golden torc. They were more long-lived than the upland racial fragment, the Firvulag (q.v.), and had a more sophisticated culture, with chivalric aspects. Their science establishment was decadent, but they retained a higher level of technoeconomy than the Firvulag. They were a spendid-looking people, graceful and stately in demeanor, fond of games, partying, music and dance, the Hunt (q.v.), and sexual adventuring. A dark taint of reckless violence clouded their magnificent image. On Pliocene Earth, their reproduction was seriously impaired by solar radiation, and the population increased very slowly (compared to that of the more fertile Firvulag). They first used ramapithecine apes as surrogate mothers, nurturing the fragile Tanu embryos. Later, time-traveling humans were used in a more successful breeding scheme, the Tanu-human hybrid having a generally Tanu appearance, but more physical vigor. It has been speculated that the Tanu-human strain persisted on Earth through the Ice Ages and contributed to the abrupt rise of Cro-Magnon humanity, through mating with Neanderthalers. Some Milieu anthropologists believe that the aboriginal Guanches of the Canary Islands, who numbered tall, blond individuals among them, represented a relict population of the ancient Tanu-humans. Others attribute an especially strong Tanu heritage to the Celts, citing mythological parallels as well as strong genes for metapsychic traits among the people.

TARASIAH (tah-rah-SY-uh) a Tanu city in northeastern Koneyn, known for textiles. The plains around the city supported great flocks of human-imported sheep and cashmere goats. Silkworm farming was also an important industry, with ramas doing most of the labor. The few synthetic-fabric manufacturing devices brought to the Pliocene by time-travelers were taken to Tarasiah. The city was ruled by the First Comer, Thufan Thunderhead, until Nodonn's final defeat. Aiken nominated Ferdiet the Courteous as City-Lord.

TASHA-BYBAR   *See* Astaurova, Anastasya.

TAT (tah't)   nom d'exil of Tatsuji Suzuki, friend to Yosh Watanabe and fellow ronin. He was killed on the abortive caravan trip to Finiah.

TATSOL FLAMESPITTER (TAH't-sawl)   a "wild" Firvulag ogre of the Maritime Alps.

TAU-FIELD   one of the primary aspects of reality, a dynamic field intimately bound into the temporal dimensions of "normal" space-time. In its purer manifestation it formed a superficies admitting time-travelers to an analogous gray limbo "hypertime," from which they were delivered into the Pliocene Epoch of Earth's distant past. *See also* Guderian Tau-Field Generator.

TAU-LATTICE   a dynamic-field construct generating time upon the spatial lattices. *See also* Lattice; Dynamic Field.

TÉ (tay)   *See* Goddess.

TÉAH (TAY-uh)   *See* Goddess.

TEICHMAN, RIKI   a member of Ocala's third generation, the five-year-old son of Sara Teichman and Guy Laroche.

TEILHARD DE CHARDIN, PIERRE (tay-AH'r d'shar-DANg)   Jesuit priest, paleontologist, and philosopher, born 1881 in the French Auvergne, died 1955 in New York City. He was one of the discoverers of Peking Man; but his most lasting fame rests upon his courageous attempt to synthesize natural science with a Christocentric theology, which produced a remarkable new vision of humanity in the universe and celebrated evolution—which he said "is a general condition to which all theories, all hypotheses, all systems must bow and which they must satisfy if they are to be thinkable and true." The Catholic Church authorities of his day were suspicious of his philosophy and he was silenced, enjoined from public discussion of his philosophy. Only his paleontological papers were officially cleared for publication during his lifetime. Teilhard submitted obediently to this censorship; but his host of friends encouraged him to refine his speculations, and after his death his books were widely circulated. The ideas of Teilhard found a ready audience among scientific philosophers of widely differing religious background. His work is at once evolutionary, synthetic, and Romantic—with a great optimism for the human future. His critics have complained that he flirts with pantheism; but careful study of his writings revealed a view of the Omega that was quite acceptable to the Catholic theology of the late twentieth century. Some of Teilhard's most important books are listed in the Bibliography of this *Pliocene Companion*, since the author of the Saga derived much of her "Milieu" from Teilhard's own. He died before the exploration of space began, but the metapsychic core of his thinking and his bold, enormous vision of humanity ensures him a place among the saints of the coming Galactic Age.

TELEVIEW   a communication terminal with optional Tri-D screen, in common use during the Milieu.

TETROL BONECRUSHER (TEH't-rawl)   Firvulag ogre and battle-champion, a member of the Gnomish Council, defeated by Alberonn in the Heroic Encounters of the Last Grand Combat.

THAGDAL, KING (THAH'g-dah'l) monarch of the Tanu for some 2000 years before the advent of Group Green to the Pliocene, he was born on the planet Duat. His sovereignty was based upon his peerless germ plasm and he sired 11,058 children, not all of them born on Earth. His eldest surviving child was Eadone, Dean of Guilds. Another elder child was Minanonn. Thagdal's three queens were Boanda, Anéar-Ia, and Nontusvel (qq.v.), the last the mother of the famous Host, who reigned with him until the Flood. Thagdal was a doughty proponent of the battle-religion, even though his own fighting days were past. He last took to the field on Duat, when both Tanu and Firvulag militants were defeated by daughter-world forces that were determined that the bad old days would not be resurrected. The remnant of Tanu and Firvulag, led by Thagdal and Yeochee I, went to a remote solar system called Void's Edge intent upon mass ritual suicide. They were persuaded to go to the Milky Way by Brede. On Earth, Thagdal was a paternal and conscientious administrator. When the first human time-travelers came, he immediately saw the advantage Milieu technology would give to the decadent Tanu science establishment. He encouraged the human mating scheme and ignored warnings from Nodonn and other traditionalists, who told him that human influence was overwhelming the Tanu heritage.

THONGSA pilot and physician among Basil's Bastards born in Xizang (Tibet) on Elder Earth. He was strongly suspected of conniving to steal an aircraft at the Ship's Grave.

THOR infant son of Stein Oleson and Sukey Davies.

THUFAN THUNDERHEAD (thoo-FAH'n) City-Lord of Tarasiah and First Comer, an adherent of Celadeyr and the other conservative Tanu who rallied round the returning Nodonn. Thufan piloted one of the flyers bringing Nodonn's invasion force to Goriah. He died when the aircraft was brought down by Aiken-Lugonn.

THULE an "Icelandic" planet in the Human Polity.

TIME-GATE or TIME-PORTAL names given to the superficies of a tau-field (q.v.).

TIMES OF UNREST a historical period some 500 years prior to the coming of Group Green to the Pliocene, during which Minanonn and the militants of his Peace Faction actively opposed the battle-religion and the Tanu throne. Nodonn and other stalwarts of the Host put down the heresy and Minanonn was exiled.

TINE the name of two glaciers on Monte Rosa—West Tine and Middle Tine.

TINY TIM nom d'exil of a silver-torc associate of Tony Wayland in Finiah, prior to its invasion.

TIRONE HEARTSINGER (tih-ROH'n) wife to Bleyn the Champion, a redactor and creator. She was the sister of Eadnar of Rocilan.

TITIRIDION (TYT-ih-rih-dee-un) a product of Milieu technology, a substance composed of titanium, iridium, and organic components, spun into extremely fine, tough fibers and used for cables, cargo nets, and the like.

TORC (tork) a necklet formed of two thick twisted strands, hinged in the back and fastening at the front with an ornate, knobbed catch. The Tanu torc was filled with psychoamplifying components and was in use in the Duat Galaxy for thousands of years by the original Tanu and by their descendants, the hybrid population of the daughter-worlds. A latent wearing the torc immediately experienced a growing operancy of the formerly unusable metafunctions. Full operancy (and dependency upon the torc) took place over several weeks, after which time it was ordinarily fatal to remove the device. A certain percentage of latents who wore the torc were incompatible and either became insane or died. *See also* Black-Torc for the maladaptation syndrome among children. The rama torcs were developed by Gomnol (q.v.) and used to enslave time-travelers. Eventually, it was discovered that torcs could be removed by severing them with an iron tool—a process that was excruciatingly painful but not usually lethal. It is fascinating to note the sacred symbolism of the torc among the ancient Gaelic peoples. Statues of their gods wore torcs, and warriors wore them in battle (e.g., the noted sculpture, *The Dying Gaul*).

TORREJON, MARIALENA   Lowlife victualer in chief at Hidden Springs, a member of the village Steering Committee. She was a great and good friend of Chief Burke.

TRANSLATION, HYPERSPATIAL   the proper term for superluminal or faster-than-light travel through hyperspace. *See* the fourth Appendix to *The Adversary*.

TRANSLATION, TEMPORAL   the proper term for time-travel. *See also* Guderian Tau-Field Generator.

TRAVIS, BENJAMIN BARRETT "BRAZOS BEN"   a chaliko trainer at Goriah, first under Nodonn and later under Aiken-Lugonn.

TRAVIS, SALLY MAE   wife to Benjamin B. Travis.

TREONET (tray-uh-NEH't)   a creator of Afaliah, a keen fancier of Milieu electronic equipment. He perished in the Flood. Later, Yosh Watanabe used his lab.

TREVARTHEN   human worker at the Amalizan gold mines, later at the Fennoscandian dysprosium diggings.

TRI-D   a television set having a three-dimensional image.

TRISKELION a figure composed of three human legs, bent at the knee and radiating from a single center, used as the heraldic cognizance of Minanonn.

TRØNDELAG a "Norse" planet of the Human Polity.

TRUAX, AUDREY ex-Rebel at Ocala, second wife to Jordan Kramer, mother of Margaret and Rebecca Kramer.

TRUCE a one-month interval preceding and following the Grand Combat, when Tanu and Firvulag eschewed hostilities.

TRUDI ex-Rebel at Ocala, nurse to Hagen and other youngsters, deceased by the time Group Green arrived in the Pliocene.

TRUMPET, THE Pliocene constellation rising ahead of the Pleiades. One of its stars, the Mouthpiece, marked the position of the Duat Galaxy. The Mouthpiece culminates at midnight on the first day of the Grand Combat.

TSL initials for terrain-scanning laser, a navigation device on certain Milieu ground vehicles.

TUAMOTU a "Polynesian" planet in the Human Polity.

TULLY a gray-torc interviewer at Castle Gateway who dealt with Group Green upon its arrival in the Pliocene.

UNITY   coadunate metapsychic minds within a specialized conjunction, the fundamental operating principle of the Galactic Milieu; a form of mutualism involving harmonious mental operation with a minimum of stress, the most perfect form of social intercourse known. Coadunation and Unity are not synonymous. The former can be deficient, in process; the latter implies a consonant mental relationship among a very large number of metapsychics (10 thousand million is the usual minimum) that generates a fully functional new entity, the Planetary (World) Mind, which may grow to be a Galactic Mind as more planets attain Unity. At the time of the Intervention, the Galactic Mind of the Milky Way included five races who had attained Unity among a majority of their populations. The human race was progressing in its first feeble steps toward coadunation; but we did not attain genuine Unity until after the Rebellion, for reasons made clear in the Milieu Trilogy. Individual minds do not lose their identity within the Unity. In a mysterious way, fully understood only by the metapsychics themselves, Unity actually enhances one's feeling of identity and self-worth. *See also* Coadunation; Mind.

UNIVERSAL FIELD THEORY   a mathematical expression of the organization of the universe, deriving all phenomena and structure from the interaction of dynamic fields in constructs called lattices. It bears scant resemblance to Einstein's pioneering efforts toward a unified field theory, but rather has its roots in the work of William A. Tiller and others active in the latter two decades of the twentieth century. The author of the Saga admits that she is incompetent to explicate fully on this theme, even though its applications and jargon permeate the Saga and Milieu Trilogy. *See also* Dynamic Field; Lattice; Mind.

UNST STARPORT   one of the main interstellar ports of entry on Earth, situated on the northernmost of the Shetland Islands.

UPSILON-FIELD   one of the primary aspects of reality, a dynamic field intimately bound into the spatial dimensions of "normal" space-time. In its purest manifestation it formed a superficies or "gate" into hyperspace that would be utilized in superluminal transport, or d-jumping. Passing through an upsilon-field was normally painful to a sentient organsim. (But *see* Mitigator.) Upsilon-field generators were among the most important devices given to Earth scientists by the Milieu following the Intervention. For a discussion of hyperspatial translation and d-jumping, *see also* the fourth Appendix to *The Adversary*.

URIET (oo-ree-ET)   adult son of Celadeyr of Afaliah and brother to Fethneya. After the Flood the pair were only nominally loyal to their traditionalist father.

UWE   *See* Guldenzopf, Uwe.

VALE OF HYENAS a deep canyon on a tributary of the Pliktol River where the Lowlives hid two exotic flying machines.

VANDA-JO Lowlife engineer of Hidden Springs, a member of the village Steering Committee, in charge of civil engineering projects.

VANIER, STEVEN ex-Rebel of Ocala, father of Raissa Vanier, former tactical analyst, who became second mate on Kyllikki.

VAN WYK, GERRIT "GERRY" ex-Rebel at Ocala, former magnate of the Concilium, a psychophysicist and colleague of Jordan Kramer. He helped Kramer and Marc Remillard design the first CE rig. His prime metafaculty was creativity.

VAR-MESK (VAH'r-meh'sk) a small Tanu city at the foot of the Maritime Alps on the River Var, originally settled by the Firvulag and taken over by Tanu during the Times of Unrest. It had trona mines and a large glass factory. The name, in Firvulag dialect, means "Stinking River Town."

VAR RIVER *See* Var-Mesk.

VARYA a cultural anthropologist in the Milieu, former colleague and lover of Bryan Grenfell.

VELTEYN (veh'l-TAY'n) City-Lord of Finiah, member of the Host, a powerful creator and psychokinetic who felt himself disgraced when Lowlives and Firvulag destroyed his city. He was designated by Mercy to lead the Creator Battalion in the Last Grand Combat, where his rash behavior led to his doom.

VENG HONG Lowlife miner at Iron Maiden village, killed by Howlers.

VERRUL (VEH'r-ool) an animal indigenous to the planet Acadie, resembling a long-legged ceratopsian rhino. It was used as a mount in ring-hockey games. Felice's taming of a verrul gave her entry into the sport.

VESTIBULUM in metapsychology, the outermost "social" aspect of an operant's mind.

VILKAS (VEEL-kah's) meaning "wolf" in Lithuanian, the nom d'exil of a man who was first a gray-torc non-commissioned officer in Finiah, and later a de-torced refugee who attached himself to Yosh Watanabe, becoming his ashigaru or man-at-arms.

VITREDUR (VIH-tr'door) a glassy material, very hard and tough, widely used in the Milieu in construction and manufacturing. It took a keen edge and was esteemed for blades.

VOICEWRITER   a recording device, with a built-in transcriber, that printed either on plaque-books or reusable durofilm sheets.

VOID'S EDGE   a small star system in the Duat Galaxy near the tip of one spiral arm. Its only habitable planet, Void's End, was the site of the aborted Nightfall War fought by the remnant of reactionary Tanu and Firvulag after they were chased off their native world. It was here that Brede proposed taking the battle-religionists to exile in another galaxy.

VOLHYNIA   a "Russo" planet of the Human Polity.

VOORHEES, EVELYN   older sister of Richard, commander of a diplomatic courier starship.

VOORHEES, FARNUM   older brother of Richard, an executive officer on a colonization starship.

VOORHEES, RICHARD   former starship master, native of the "American" planet Assawompset, who came to the Pliocene after being convicted of violating the Altruism Statutes and after losing his means of livelihood. His adventures are detailed in *The Many-Colored Land*.

VOSGES (VOH'zh)   in the Milieu, a heavily forested range of low mountains lying west of the Rhine. Its highest eminence is Grand Ballon, 1423 meters. The Alsatian Vosges have a folkloric mystique similar to that of the Black Forest on the opposite side of the Rhine Graben, to which the range is geologically linked. Both regions were famed in early days as a haunt of monsters, goblins, and the like. A Celtic shrine to Lugh, later a Roman temple to Mercury, was built on one of the peaks, le Donon. In the Pliocene, the Vosges was more rugged, a refuge of Lowlife outlaws amid a concentration of Firvulag settlements. The Firvulag capital of High Vrazel was on Grand Ballon.

VRENOL (v'REE-noh'l)   a young Tanu stalwart of Goriah, Hunting companion of Nodonn.

VRENTI   a Lowlife killed by Howlers on the first iron-seeking expedition.

VULCAN   one of the Lowlife Iron Villages of the Moselle River.

WALDEMAR, CAPTAL gray-torc noncommissioned officer in charge of Lady Epone's caravan to Finiah.

WANG, CAPTAL officer of the watch on the night of Finiah's invasion.

WANG, MISS nom d'exil of Priscilla Sui-Chi Wang; in the Milieu a commercial starship captain, she became one of Basil's Bastards.

WARBURTON, PONGO former rhocraft pilot in the Milieu, one of Basil's Bastards.

WARRIOR OGRESS a member of the female fighting force of the Mighty Ayfa, later Queen of Firvulag.

WARSHAW, CORDELIA ex-Rebel at Ocala, former magnate of the Concilium, in the Milieu a psychotactician and xenologist. During Marc's long "absences" on his Pliocene star-search, she was the principal administrator of the loosely organized Ocala colony. Her only child was Marlys, and her grandson was Davey.

WARSHAW, DAVEY   a member of Ocala's third generation, the six-year-old son of Marlys Warshaw and Guy Laroche.

WATANABE, YOSHIMITSU "YOSH" or "YOSHI-SAMA" (wah-tah-nah-bay, yoh-shee-mih-t'soo)   former robotics engineer of Denver CO on Elder Earth who came to the Pliocene with his friend Tat planning to live the life of a Japanese ronin. He became an associate of King Aiken-Lugonn and was granted an honorary golden torc. His adventures are told in *The Many-Colored Land*, *The Nonborn King*, and *The Adversary*.

WATER CAVES   inundated caverns beneath the Feldberg, part of Sugoll's realm. They were a source of the Ystroll, the Proto-Danube of the Pliocene, and also gave rise to the Paradise River near Finiah and a south-flowing tributary of the Rhine.

WAYLAND, ANTHONY BRYCE "TONY," called WAYLAND-VELKONN (vel-KAH'n)   metallurgical engineer, formerly a silver-torc in charge of the barium extraction operation at Finiah, later a reluctant worker in the Iron Villages and in the Guderian Project of Aiken-Lugonn. His adventures are told in *The Nonborn King* and *The Adversary*.

WEB, RHO-FIELD   the visible manifestation of the rhofield (q.v.) that clothes the skin of an aircraft. It resembles a crawling network of dim purplish fire.

WELL OF THE SEA   a spring of potable water rising in the White Silver Plain below Muriah, it bisected the ritual battlefield of the Grand Combat.

WERNER   human prisoner of the Firvulag at devastated Bardelask.

WESSEX   a "British" planet of the Human Polity.

WESTERN OCEAN the Atlantic of the Pliocene.

WEX-VELITOKAL *See* Candyman, Bert.

WHITE SILVER PLAIN a salt flat lying south of Muriah, scene of the Tanu-sponsored Grand Combats, as described in *The Golden Torc*. The Plain is mentioned in an ancient Celtic poem quoted in the first Appendix to *The Many-Colored Land*.

WIGGY a human teamster near Roniah.

WIMBORNE, BASIL former professor of Latin literature at the University of Oxford, and mountaineer. He was in the Finiah caravan, together with four members of Group Green. After the prisoner revolt, he led one contingent of escapees who fled in boats on the Lac de Bresse. He and his companions were soon recaptured and held in the Finiah dungeons until the city fell. After this he participated in the invasion of the torc works in Muriah, where he was again captured. Freed by Brede, he was a close companion of Elizabeth, Amerie, and Chief Burke on the Aven exodus. Later he led a group of some thirty daredevils (*see* Basil's Bastards) on the second Ship's Grave expedition. His great ambition was to climb the highest mountain in the Pliocene, and to this end he had been rejuvenated and had his muscles, heart, and lungs strengthened, which gave him great stamina.

WORLD MIND *See* Mind.

WYLIE, JASMIN a member of Ocala's second generation, the daughter of Olivia Wylie and Abdulkadir Al-Mahmoud.

WYLIE, OLIVIA ex-Rebel of Ocala, the wife of Abdulkadir Al-Mahmoud and mother of Jasmin Wylie.

X-LASER   a powerful photonic weapon capable of penetrating the strongest portable sigma-field screen. The only X-lasers in the Pliocene were those installed around Marc Remillard's star-search observatory on Ocala, which were later taken aboard Kyllikki for use against Aiken-Lugonn's Guderian Project. X-lasers were the only Pliocene weapons—other than blasters—having the photonic beam jacketed in a dynamic-field "sleeve" that precluded atmospheric (or human-instigated) interference.

YBAAR (ee-BAH'r)   Tanu name for the Proto-Ebro River in Spain.

YEOCHEE IV, KING (YEE-oh-chee)   monarch of the Firvulag nation at the time of Group Green's advent to the Pliocene. He was known as a peaceable "caretaker" king who had the unenviable job of reigning during the Tanu domination of the Grand Combat. His term of elected office was due to end at the finale of the Last Grand Combat. He and his Queen, Klahnino, were among the few Firvulag to perish in the Flood, since they remained to witness the contest between Nodonn and Aiken following the Combat proper. Most of the other Little People had already taken ship for home on the Great Lagoon when the Flood wave struck.

YEVGENY   a silver-torc associate of Tony Wayland in Finiah prior to its invasion.

YLAHAYLL (IH'l-uh-hay'l)   contumelious exclamation in Firvulag dialect meaning "bad luck to [you]." Oddly enough, the same word with the same meaning resurfaced in Elizabethan English.

YOSH   *See* Watanabe, Yoshimitsu.

YOTUNAG (YOH-tuh-nah'g)   a savage tribe of gigantic Howlers living in Fennoscandia. They were cannibals.

YSAAR (ee-SAH'r)   a river flowing adjacent to Bardelask, a tributary of the Pliocene Rhône. It is analogous to the modern Isère.

YSEZ (ee-SEH'z)   a small river, east of the Gresson, flowing southward from the Helvetides. It is comparable to the modern Sésia.

YSTRÓLL (ee-STROH'l)   the Howler name for the Pliocene Proto-Danube, meaning "Great Brown River."

YUCHOR TIDYPAW (YOO-chaw'r)   president of the Firvulag Guild of Gemcutters, in charge of producing the Singing Stone.

ZAP   to hit or strike with a beam or bolt of energy, such as a laser beam, lightning stroke, or psychocreative emanation. The verb first came into general use during the latter part of the twentieth century.

ZAPPER   Milieu slang term for any weapon projecting a coherent beam of light or other photonic radiation. There are many types ranging from light-pistols to great photon cannons. The most powerful, such as the X-lasers and so-called blasters, have the beam jacketed by a dynamic field to minimize atmospheric fouling and plasmatization at the point of impact. Zappers used in the Saga include the popular Matsushita RL-9 red-laser carbine, which had a beam dialable from needle to blade and a range of about 320 meters in clear air; the Weatherby Y-42, a higher-powered long gun utilizing yellow light; the solar-powered Mauser; the Bosch 414 blaster, using a jacketed blue-white beam; and the X-lasers of Marc Remillard's Ocala observatory. The Spear and the Sword were also zappers.

ZDENKO   captal in the escort of Lord Creyn to Roniah.

ZOO ISLAND   a game preserve established by ex-Rebels in the Bermoothes.

ZORCH   Milieu slang combining "zap" and "scorch," meaning "to blast with exceeding thoroughness," either mentally or with a light-weapon.

A Chronology
of the Saga

~~~~~~~~~~~~~~~~~~~~~~~~~~~

A Chronology
of the Saga

2013 — The Great Intervention
2014 — Birth of Paul Remillard, "The Man Who Sold New Hampshire"
2034 — Invention of Guderian Tau-Generator (time-gate)
2038 — Birth of Marc Remillard
2041 — Death of Professor Guderian; translation of first time-traveler; establishment of l'Auberge du Portail
2080 — Birth of Hagen Remillard
2082 — Birth of Cloud Remillard
2083 — Metapsychic Rebellion; Marc and ex-Rebels enter Pliocene
2106 — Madame Guderian enters Pliocene
2110 — *15 May:* Mercy Lamballe enters Pliocene
20 August: Group Green arrives Auberge
25 August: Group Green enters Pliocene
26 August: Northern Party Group Green in caravan; Southern Party travels the Rhône to Darask
27 August: Lady Epone slain; prisoners escape. Baby Epone born with help of Elizabeth

2101 — *28 August* Amerie breaks arm; Basil and most of prisoners recaptured; Sukey helps to heal Stein's mind

29 August: Southern Party descends Glissade; Northerners taken by Mme. Guderian's Low-lives

30 August: Northern party flees to Tree; Southern Party arrives Muriah, banquets with Tanu royalty

31 August: Northern Party has great conference in Tree; Bryan meets Gomnol; Elizabeth meets Brede; Sukey meets Tasha-Bybar; Tasha meets Stein

1 September: Northern Party visits King Yeochee, sets out for Ship's Grave; Aiken and Stein begin martial training

6 September: Northern Party crosses Rhine

10 September: Northern Party reaches Fungus Forest

15 September: Stein and Aiken at September Sport Meeting, initiated into battle-company

17 September: Northern Party reaches Black Forest crest; Delbaeth Quest leaves Muriah for Koneyn mainland

18 September: Northern Party meets Sugoll

22 September: Northern Party arrives at Ship's Grave

26 September: Richard tests flyer

27 September: Aiken and Stein enter Delbaeth's cave

29 September: Aiken attacks Delbaeth; flyer arrives at Hidden Springs

30 September: Finiah attacked at dawn

1 October: Truce begins at dawn; Finiah withdrawal

3 October: Felice prowls ruins of Finiah

7 October: Madame at the refugee camp near

2110 — Rhine; Exalteds view time-gate; Mr. Betsy arrives in Pliocene

8 October: The torc-works sabotage party leaves Hidden Springs

10 October: Elizabeth raises Brede to operancy

14 October: The Northern Party arrives at Roniah Fair

15 October: Madame contacts Elizabeth and Aiken

20 October: The saboteurs arrive in Muriah

22 October: Torc works attacked; Madame and Claude at the time-portal

30 October: Elizabeth's balloon leaves Muriah

31 October: Grand Combat Day 1

1 November: Grand Combat Day 2; Felice at Gibraltar

2 November: Grand Combat Day 3

3 November: Grand Combat Day 4

4 November: Grand Combat Day 5: the Flood

5 November: Aftermath

9 November: Exodus from Aven begins

3 December: Aiken and Mercy arrive Goriah

14 December: Howlers ask Gnomish Council for franchise

15 December: Sharn and Ayfa elected co-monarchs of Firvulag

2111 — *6 January*: Howlers send letter to High Vrazel re Grand Loving

4 February: Firvulag attack and devastate Burask

2 March: Culluket arrives Goriah, becomes Aiken's confidant

13 March: In Ocala, Marc begins fishing

20 March: Meteor shower marks end of European rainy season

22 March: Firvulag attack Iron Maiden village; exodus ends at Lac Provençal

2111 — *24 March*: Elizabeth arrives at Black Crag

25 March: Sullivan and Olone arrive Goriah

30 March: Howler migration begins

31 March: On Kersic, Huldah watches in vain for Tanu Hunt

2 April: Fian and Kuhal struggle in Africa

3 April: Yosh meets Jim and Vilkas

4 April: Aiken shows off Grand Loving preparations

5 April: Fian dies

6 April: "Devils" talk to Felice

7 April: Elizabeth observes the ex-Rebels

8 April: Aiken leaves on his Progress

9 April: Burke and Amerie meet Anatoly at Castle Gateway

10 April: Cloud's party leaves Ocala for Europe

12 April: Aiken at Afaliah

15 April: Agraynel born

18 April: Nodonn awakes

19 April: Burke meets troublesome refugees at Lac de Bresse

20 April: Tony and Dougal taken to Nionel

21 April: Aiken returns to Goriah

27 April: Cloud's party arrives in Spain

28 April: King Sharn learns to Hunt

30 April: Grand Loving of Firvulag begins at dawn; Tanu Grand Loving Night of Secret Love

1 May: Tanu weddings at noon; Nodonn regains his power

2 May: Aiken crowned King of Many-Colored Land; Nodonn calls to Mercy

12 May: The rest of second generation flees Ocala

16 May: Marc returns from star-search

17 May: Felice comes to Elizabeth on Black Crag

26 May: Aiken talks to Marc via farspeech

27 May: Fleeing Children of Rebellion forced to Africa; Nodonn arrives Var-Mesk

2111 — *2 June*: Burke, Amerie, and party arrive Hidden Springs; Felice attains sanity; Aiken's fleet arrives Río Genil

3 June: Felice visits Amerie; Aiken, Marc, and their forces encounter Felice at Río Genil; Marc goes into regen-tank

9 June: Aiken wakes restored

15 June: Basil's Bastards arrive Ship's Grave

16 June: Mercy and Celadeyr meet Nodonn at Var-Mesk

20 July: Basil's Bastards hide aircraft on Monte Rosa

22 July: Cloud and Kuhal heal together in Afaliah

30 July: Mercy returns to Aiken in Goriah

19 August: Kite tests near Goriah

22 August: Tony Wayland in High Vrazel; Sharn contacts Nodonn; Children of Rebellion prepare to cross Rif

23 August: Marc exits the tank

24 August: Nodonn secures flyers; Bastards imprisoned in Afaliah

25 August: *First Anniversary Group Green arrival*. Aiken confronts Nodonn; the Fog; Children at Waterfall

26 August: Bastards awake in Afaliah dungeon; Anatoly goes to Black Crag; Elizabeth sees vision of Marc

28 August: Bardelask falls; Tony Wayland goes free

1 September: Marc and ex-Rebels leave Ocala in Kyllikki; Basil's Bastards leave Afaliah

2 September: Aiken confronts Hagen's party; Elizabeth attempts to redact Brendan

3 September: Burke goes hunting; Sharn holds maneuvers; Tony leaves Bardelask; Aiken, Children, and Bastards leave Calamosk

5 September: Aiken in Quicksilver Cave

2111 — *6 September*: Alps expedition sets out for Darask
   7 September: Kyllikki 400 km SW Bermuda
   8 September: Alps Expedition leaves Darask
   12 September: Aiken returns to Goriah; a bad night on Kyllikki
   13 September: Marc seen by Aiken in Goriah; Marc at Black Crag
   20 September: Alps expedition approaches Monte Rosa; Kyllikki 1800 km W Azores
   22 September: Conference at Camp Bettaforca
   24 September: Brendan is cured
   25 September: Hidden Springs abandoned; Hagen's group attacks Aiken; Camp 1 set up on Rosa
   27 September: Tony taken by Burke; Basil sets up Camp 2
   28 September: Camp 3 set up on Rosa
   29 September: Assault teams begin Rosa climb; Famorel attacks; Burke brings Tony to Roniah
   30 September: Firvulag attack Roniah; fighting at Camp Bettaforca; assault teams reach Camp 2
   1 October: Truce begins at dawn; storm on Rosa; assault team at Camp 3
   2 October: Assault team crosses col and reaches aircraft
   4 October: Basil departs for summit
   6 October: Basil on summit
   8 October: Minanonn takes Elizabeth to Goriah
   9 October: Sharn receives Sword at Nionel; Kyllikki in Gulf of Armorica; Aiken, Hagen, and Cloud meet Marc at Black Crag
   11 October: Marc's deadline
   15 October: Aiken demonstrates aircraft at Roniah Fair, Burke begins search for Kyllikki
   23 October: Burke finds Kyllikki; attack at Fennoscandian mine; the mutiny
   24 October: Kyllikki sent to Goriah; mass redaction begins
   28 October: Kyllikki arrives Goriah

2111 — *30 October*: Mass redaction complete; Black Crag evacuated

31 October: Day 1 of Grand Tourney

1 November: Day 2 of Grand Tourney

2 November: Day 3 of Grand Tourney

3 November: Day 4 of Grand Tourney

4 November: Day 5 of Grand Tourney; Nightfall

5 November: Tony returns to Nionel

8 November: The time-gate closes

14 December: Gaudete Sunday in the Synchronous Milieu and the Duat Galaxy

The Remillard
Family Tree

The Remillard

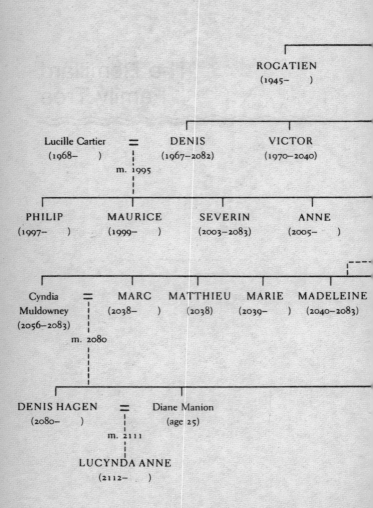

ROGATIEN
(1945–)

Lucille Cartier   =   DENIS   VICTOR
(1968–)   (1967–2082)   (1970–2040)
         m. 1995

PHILIP   MAURICE   SEVERIN   ANNE
(1997–)   (1999–)   (2003–2083)   (2005–)

Cyndia   =   MARC   MATTHIEU   MARIE   MADELEINE
Muldowney   (2038–)   (2038)   (2039–)   (2040–2083)
(2056–2083)
         m. 2080

DENIS HAGEN   =   Diane Manion
(2080–)   (age 25)
         m. 2111

LUCYNDA ANNE
(2112–)

Family Tree

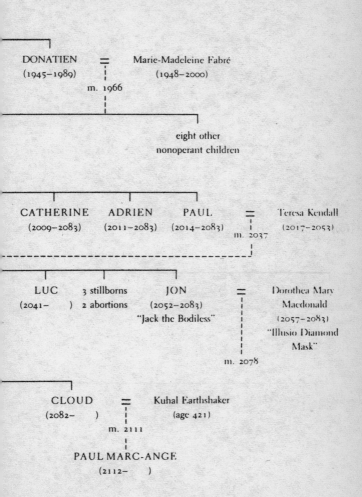

DONATIEN = Marie-Madeleine Fabré
(1945–1989)   (1948–2000)
    m. 1966

eight other
nonoperant children

CATHERINE   ADRIEN   PAUL = Teresa Kendall
(2009–2083)   (2011–2083)   (2014–2083)   (2017–2053)
    m. 2037

LUC   3 stillborns   JON = Dorothea Mary
(2041–)   2 abortions   (2052–2083)   Macdonald
    "Jack the Bodiless"   (2057–2083)
    "Illusio Diamond
    Mask"
    m. 2078

CLOUD = Kuhal Earthshaker
(2082–)   (age 421)
    m. 2111

PAUL MARC-ANGE
(2112–)

The Ocala Rebels
and Their Offspring

The Ocala Rebels
and Their Offspring

IN THE PROLOGUE TO *The Nonborn King*, one reads that farsensors of the Roniah City-Lord Bormol discerned 101 operant human beings among the invaders who had unexpectedly come through at Castle Gateway; these presumably included the infants Hagen and Cloud Remillard, together with their father Marc and 98 defeated insurgents of the Metapsychic Rebellion.

Some twenty-seven years later, when the action of the Saga began, the population of ex-Rebels had diminished to forty-three aging conspirators, plus Marc. In addition, there were thirty-two adult children in the second generation and five youngsters in the third.

The following lists give the people of Ocala and their affinities, at the time of Felice's rupture of Gibraltar. When a mate or a parent is not given, the person should be presumed deceased before the Flood. There were also other second-generation children deceased, and two babies of the third generation who did not survive.

MAGNATES OF THE CONCILIUM

Marc Remillard—father of Hagen and Cloud Remillard
Alexis Manion—father of Diane Manion
Owen Blanchard—no offspring
Helayne Strangford—mother of Christopher Strangford
Jeffrey Steinbrenner—no offspring
Jordan Kramer—husband of Audrey Truax, father of
  Margaret and Rebecca Kramer
Ragnar Gathen—father of Elaby Gathen
Patricia Castellane—no offspring
Peter Paul Dalembert—father of Barry Dalembert
Cordelia Warshaw—mother of Marlys Warshaw
Gerrit Van Wyk—no offspring
Diarmid Keogh—brother and husband to Dierdre, father
  of Nial
Dierdre Keogh—sister and wife to Diarmid, mother of
  Nial

SUBORDINATE GRAND MASTERS

Isobel Layton—wife of Alonzo Jarrow, mother of Vaughn
  Jarrow
Alonzo Layton—husband of Isobel Layton, father of
  Vaughn Jarrow
Dorsey Kodama—husband of Midori Kuwada, father of
  Fumiko Kodama
Midori Kuwada—wife of Dorsey Kodama, mother of
  Fumiko Kodama
Lu-Shen Chan—husband of Frieda Singer-Dow, father of
  Chee-Wu Chan
Frieda Singer-Dow—wife of Lu-Shen Chan, mother of
  Chee-Wu Chan
Olivia Wylie—wife of Abdulkadir Al-Mahmoud, mother
  of Jasmin Wylie
Abdulkadir Al-Mahmoud—husband of Olivia Wylie,
  father of Jasmin Wylie

Nanomea Fox—lover of Eva Smuts, mother of Kané Fox-Laroche

Eva Smuts—lover of Nanomea Fox, co-mother of Kané Fox-Laroche

Allison Sherwoode—mother of André Sherwoode-Laroche

Guy "Boom-Boom" Laroche—father of Kané Fox-Laroche, André Sherwoode-Laroche, Riki Teichman, and Davey Warshaw

Walter Saastamoinen—father of Veikko Saastamoinen

Heather Jacoby—mother of Leila Jacoby

Audrey Truax—wife of Jordan Kramer, mother of Margaret and Rebecca Kramer

Claire Shaunavon—mother of Matiwilda Shaunavon

Javier Spaulding Cisneros—father of Rick Spaulding

John Horvath—father of Imre Horvath

Eileen Morgenthaler—wife of Charles Morlaix, mother of Jillian Morgenthaler

Charles Morlaix—husband to Eileen Morgenthaler, no offspring

Laura Bruce-Overton—mother of Philip Overton

Charisse Buckmaster—mother of Quinn Buckmaster

Morrison Collins—father of Lusk Collins

Arkady Petrovich O'Malley—father of Irena O'Malley

Quinn Fitzpatrick—father of Quinn Buckmaster

Steven Vanier—father of Raissa Vanier

Roy Marchand—no offspring

Arne-Rolf Lillestrom—no offspring

Everett Garrison—mate to Ronald Inman, no offspring

Ronald Inman—mate to Everett Garrison, no offspring

Gary Evans—no offspring

SECOND GENERATION

Hagen Remillard—son of Marc Remillard
Cloud Remillard—daughter of Marc Remillard
Diane Manion—daughter of Alexis Manion

Nial Keogh—son of Dierdre and Diarmid Keogh

Christopher Strangford—son of Helayne Strangford, husband of Leila Jacoby, father of Joel Strangford

Leila Jacoby—daughter of Heather Jacoby, wife of Christopher Strangford, mother of Joel Strangford

Phil Overton—son of Laura Bruce-Overton, father of Calinda Overton

Fumiko Kodama—daughter of Dorsey Kodama and Midori Kuwada, wife of Barry Dalembert, mother of Hope Dalembert

Barry Dalembert—son of Peter Dalembert, husband of Fumiko Kodama, father of Hope Dalembert

Marlys Warshaw—daughter of Cordelia Warshaw, mother of Davey Warshaw (by Guy Laroche)

Sara Teichman—mother of Riki Teichman (by Guy Laroche)

Rebecca Kramer—daughter of Jordan Kramer and Audrey Truax

Margaret Kramer—daughter of Jordan Kramer and Audrey Truax

Veikko Saastamoinen—son of Walter Saastamoinen, mate to Irena O'Malley

Chee-Wu Chan—daughter of Frieda Singer-Dow and Lu-Shen Chan

Matiwilda Shaunavon—daughter of Claire Shaunavon

Rick Spaulding—son of Javier Spaulding Cisneros

Imre Horvath—son of John Horvath

André Sherwoode-Laroche—son of Allison Sherwoode and Guy Laroche

Kané Fox-Laroche—son of Nanomea Fox and Guy Laroche

Quinn Buckmaster—son of Charisse Buckmaster and Quinn Fitzpatrick

Irena O'Malley—daughter of Arkady O'Malley, mate to Veikko Saastamoinen

Jasmin Wylie—daughter of Abdulkadir Al-Mahmoud and Olivia Wylie

Lusk Collins—son of Morrison Collins
Ramsey McQuaid—parents deceased
Marcia Matlock—parents deceased
Kurt Brandeis—parents deceased
Vaughn Jarrow—son of Alonzo Jarrow and Isobel Layton
Elaby Gathen—son of Ragnar Gathen
Jillian Morgenthaler—daughter of Eileen Morgenthaler
Kenneth Le Baron—parents deceased
Raissa Vanier—daughter of Steven Vanier

THIRD GENERATION

Davey Warshaw—son of Marlys Warshaw and Guy Laroche
Riki Teichman—son of Sara Teichman and Guy Laroche
Joel Strangford—son of Leila Jacoby and Christopher Strangford
Calinda Overton—daughter of Phil Overton
Hope Dalembert—daughter of Barry Dalembert and Fumiko Kodama

Author's Three
Original Maps
of Pliocene Europe

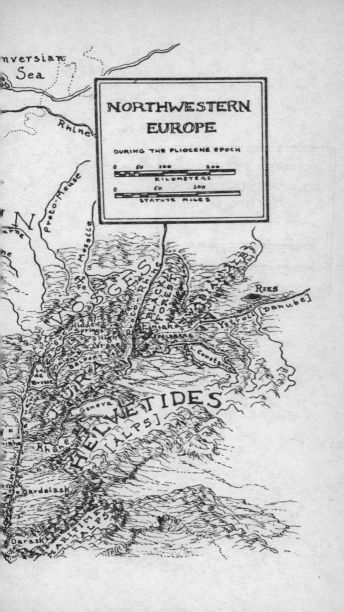

EASTERN
AVEN
[BALEARIC PENINSULA]

DURING THE PLIOCENE EPOCH

KILOMETERS

STATUTE MILES

DRAGON
RANGE

GROVES

AND

PLANTATIONS

FOREST

PRESERVES

DUNES

AND

FLATS

jm ©1980

Southern Lago

Catalan

Gulf

MURIAH
AND
ENVIRONS

PLAIN OR
DIRT PIERCERS
E SQUARES MAIN
DOCK
REDACTORS PALACE
PSYCHOKINETICS
REDACTORS CREATORS
ARENA
FAR HEALERS

WELL
TANU HOWLA GREDE'S
CAMP CAMP HOUSE
BULL
LISTS
BATTLEFIELD

RETORT

WHITE
SILVER
PLAIN

Great

Lagoon

Estuary

UTHERN

SALT

FLATS

Two Maps of
Ocala Island
and Vicinity

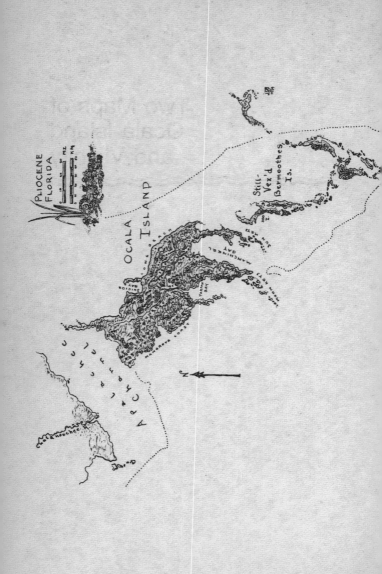

PLIOCENE
FLORIDA

OCALA ISLAND

Still-
Vex'd
Bermoothes
Is.

MANCHINEEL BAY

ARCHANGEL COAST

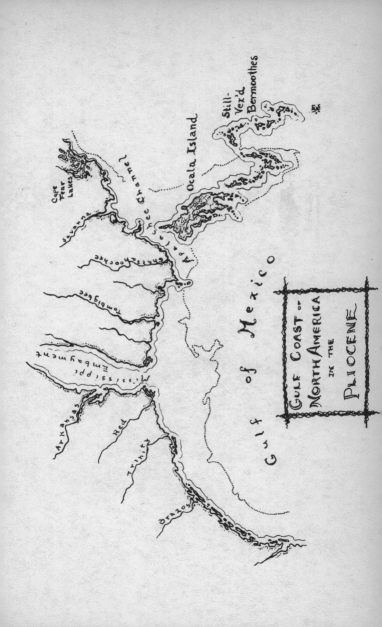

The Good Ship Kyllikki

The Good Ship Kyllikki

KYLLIKKI IS A FOUR-MASTED gaff-rigged schooner of the type that hauled timber in the late nineteenth and early twentieth century, especially along the Pacific Coast of North America. She is built mostly of wood and is alloy-sheathed below the waterline. She is fitted with solar-panel sails but carries conventional canvas as well. There is an automatic reefing system permitting one-man operation; but she can be also worked in the usual manner, entirely from the deck, by a crew of seven. She has an auxiliary electric engine driving a retractable cycloidal impeller system with twin rotors, similar to the Voith Schneider units of the late twentieth century. Kyllikki's bridge and navigation station are amidships. Marc's accommodation is in the after deckhouse, above the hold containing the CE rig.

SPECIFICATIONS

Length: 70 m (230 ft)
Beam: 17 m (56 ft)
Depth: 5 m (16.5 ft)
Draft: 6 m (20 ft)
Foremast ht: 34 m (112 ft)

Gross tons: 1100
Speed under power: 6 kts
Arms: 16 X-lasers, 30
   Bosch 414 blasters, 10
   Colt SD-15 sonic disrup-
   tors

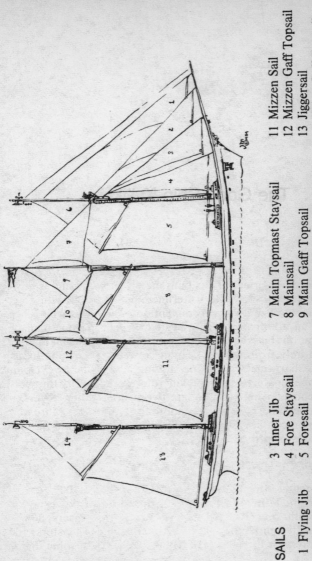

SAILS

1 Flying Jib	8 Mainsail
2 Outer Jib	9 Main Gaff Topsail
3 Inner Jib	10 Mizzen Topmast Staysail
4 Fore Staysail	11 Mizzen Sail
5 Foresail	12 Mizzen Gaff Topsail
6 Fore Gaff Topsail	13 Jiggersail
7 Main Topmast Staysail	14 Jigger Gaff Topsail

The Double
Ourobouros

The Double Ourobouros

THE TUG-OF-WAR DEVICE for the Grand Tourney is basically a huge ring passing through a "mountain" containing arrays of Van de Graaff electrostatic generators. The opposing teams mentally "tug" upward on the part called a bracelet. This causes the ring to rotate. The harder a team pulls, the farther away from the enemy serpent's mouth the tail of their own serpent will be—and conversely, the closer the tail of the enemy serpent will be to the mouth of the team's own serpent.

In this drawing, the tails are "in neutral." Part of the serpentine circle is made of nonconductive glass. In order to win, a team must draw the enemy tail's conductive section—the part with the scales, above the glass—into the serpent's mouth. Once inside, the "swallowed" enemy tail is subjected to greater and greater electrical shocks as it is drawn farther into the generator arrays. The minds of the enemy team have a more and more difficult time maintaining their grip, since their grandstand seats are connected to the electrical apparatus. When the enemy team can't stand the electricity anymore, individual members rise from their seats, resigning, and the minds let go of the bracelet.

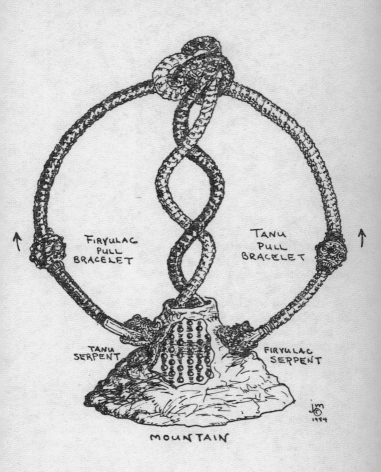

FIRYULAC
PULL
BRACELET

TANU
PULL
BRACELET

TANU
SERPENT

FIRYULAC
SERPENT

MOUNTAIN

Music in My Head—
Science Fiction
as Opera

Music in My Head—
Science Fiction as Opera

"THE TROUBLE WITH LIFE," complains a wistful middle-aged lady in an immortal Franklin Folger cartoon, "is that it has no background music."

True, true...for some people. But there are others who *do* tend to hear music in their heads as they go about their everyday activities, and especially at life's high points: when viewing a sublime landscape or special work of art, when experiencing some wild thrill in sports or outdoor adventures, when making love, when contemplating sleeping children or a well-completed job, when experiencing great sorrow or disaster, when rapt in extraordinary contemplation—or even when writing books.

I confess. I *do* hear music. I suspect it has something to do with the capricious right-brain, which in my case is stuffed with quite as much music as the left-brain is stuffed with a research library. So as I wrote the Saga, I couldn't help but hear the music that went along with it. It is, after all, an opera! In his fascinating book *Literature as Opera*, Gary Schmidgall half-seriously characterizes opera's "divorce from artistic naturalism, its gestural mode, and its stylization ... The world of opera is one of high relief, magnification, escalation." And that's my Saga, folks: perhaps not a genuine space opera in the old fannish sense, but operatic nevertheless.

There's more music besides "Londonderry Air" playing as a background to the Pliocene books. Let me tell you about it.

Perhaps the music that evokes the Many-Colored Land most closely is that of Wagner's *Ring*. Here in the Seattle area where I live we are lucky to have a summer festival each year performing the entire *Ring* Cycle. It's not Bayreuth, but it *can* be pretty damn good—especially for those with a cast-iron gluteus maximus, since you get all four operas in a single week, some fifteen hours of musical melodrama demanding a heroic cast, orchestra, and audience. The *Ring* is full of myth and passion and symbol—in the literary, musical, and visual sense—and I have used many of the same archetypes as Wagner in building my Pliocene Saga. I even stole a basic "nature" motif from the *Ring* for the Song of the Singing Stone in *The Nonborn King*. That sonorous theme, which begins *Das Rheingold* in primordial darkness and slowly focuses light on the flowing waters of the Rhine, is to me the music of the gray limbo, womblike and all-encompassing, outside of creation and yet a part of it. And then Brede's Ship breaks through...

The mystical gold of the River Rhine symbolizes power in *Rheingold*. Its theme is to me the theme of the golden torcs, those irresistible but ultimately disastrous instruments to which the mind and soul become addicted. Wagner's gold music is seductive, ecstatically sung by three fatal Lorelei creatures, who guard the treasure and warn what terrible things will happen to those spellbound by the magic Ring fashioned from it.

Das Rheingold also has music belonging to Aiken Drum. His character begins, however, with a Richard Strauss theme rather than a Wagnerian one. Aiken starts out as Till Eulenspiegel. I can hear Strauss's rollicking (ultimately catastrophic) melodies playing in the background of Aiken's activities all through *The Many-Colored Land*—and especially in *The Golden Torc* when he fights the giant crocodile. But when Aiken begins to darken and mature, his music does as well. I begin to hear the scintillant theme of Loge from *Das Rheingold*, the fire-music. Loge is not a god but an elemental, a mocker, a cynical intelligence, a Trickster. He transcends himself when he clothes sleeping Brünnhilde with magical flame at the climax of *Die Walküre* and again when, at the end of *Götterdämmerung*, he sets fire to the world. I hear Loge's music at that part of *The Adversary* when King Aiken-Lugonn finally achieves ultimate power. But when he wakes on the burnt and blasted heath the song is "Vocalise" by Rachmaninoff, and the voice is Anna Moffo's.

Wagner's *Ring* has many other wonderful themes that seem to fit the Saga. The descent of Loge and Wotan into the land of the dwarf metalcrafters is Firvulagian to the nines. Fafner's dragon sounds to me like Pallol One-Eye. The Thundergod's summoning of the storm is the descent and crash of Brede's Ship, and the entrance of the gods into Valhalla is the Great Ordeal at the Ship's Grave. Alas—the Valkyrie's Ride has become too hackneyed; so I pass it by, and let the Flying Hunt become airborne to César Franck's *Le Chasseur Maudit*. But Siegfried's Forest Murmurs paint a great picture of Pliocene jungles; and the funeral march of the hero climaxes Aiken's ultimate duel with Nodonn in the sky above Goriah.

A gentler mood of Wagner, not really a part of the *Ring*, but containing many creative themes, is the *Siegfried Idyll*. I hear it in Mercy's birth scene, when she holds Agraynel for the first time. Mercy's more ominous aspects are recalled by primal Erda's melody, heard in both major and minor variations throughout the four operas.

Leaving the *Ring*, but remaining with Wagner, I hear the horns of *The Flying Dutchman* when Richard Voorhees solos the exotic rho-craft above the crater lake. Richard and Stein dine in the Milieu for the last time outside l'Auberge du Portail, and the "subdued, jangling tune" played on the jukebox chez Louis is an up-tempo, synthesized version of "Senta's Ballad" from Act Two of *The Dutchman*.

Other characters besides Richard seem to have signature themes. Sister Amerie's is Debussy's *Le Martyre de St. Sebastien*. Civilized, doomed Bryan recalls Fauré's *Pavanne, Opus 50*. Felice's ambivalent horror seems caught by the symphonic poem, *The Noon Witch* by Antonín Dvořák. The deadly pride of Nodonn, and his futility, cries out from Rachmaninoff's *Prince Rostislav*. A lovely and terrible cantata for male choir, *The King of the Stars* by Stravinsky, has words as well as music that fit Marc Remillard. Elizabeth has no single theme, but her yearning anxiety may be suggested by the wordless choruses in Ravel's *Daphnis and Chloe*. When the Tanu Master of Guilds, Eadone, welcomes Elizabeth to Muriah, it is with the electrifying "Dulcissime" from *Carmina Burana* by Carl Orff; and the Tanu throng praise and tempt Elizabeth at the same time with Orff's "Blanziflor et Helena."

Carmina Burana has some marvelous Firvulag music, as well. The tavern dancers in Malachee's Toot dissolve in fire to "Veni, Veni, Venias." The cool veil-dancer weaves her spell with "In Trutina." At the Firvulag Grand Loving, the wedding of the loathly brides is celebrated with "Swaz hie gat umbe" and "Were diu werlt alle min." Tony Wayland and Rowane make love to "Stetit Puella."

There are many works having what I call "romantic excess" that are fine Tanu background. The fanfares from *Lohengrin* and the Entrance of the Guests from *Tannhäuser* are obvious Wagnerian bits; but one might also cite Walton's *Symphony No. 1*, Smetana's *Richard III*, and Berlioz's *Symphonie Fantastique*—especially the gruesome "Marche au supplice." His *Requiem*, oddly enough, has what I consider to be the ideal entrance antiphon for the Grand Tourney: "Tuba Mirum," which is actually about the Last Trump. (Perhaps the theme is more appropriate than I thought, after all!)

When the Raven flies over drowned Muriah, I hear Rachmaninoff again: *The Isle of the Dead*. The same music makes a reprise following the fight at the Río Genil. The journey through the Fungus Forest and the land of the Howlers is embodied in *The Mysterious Mountain* by Pacific Northwestern composer Alan Hovhaness. The final movement of that work depicts the conquest of Monte Rosa. The great schooner Kyllikki sails in accompaniment to the ¾ horn passages climaxing Sibelius's *Symphony No. 5*, and parts of Walton's *First*.

Aiken and Mercy dance after their wedding to Ravel's "La Valse," music for damned lovers; but Marc and Elizabeth's waltz is from *Der Rosenkavalier*—glorious, a tempo, and ever so subtly dissonant.

I am torn between two pieces of music for the conclusion to the Pliocene Saga. Sometimes I hear the soaring climax of Mahler's *Second*; but this, it seems to me, would be more appropriate for the end of the Milieu Trilogy. At other times I hear the last movement of Saint-Saëns' "Organ" *Symphony No. 3*—lush, romantic, and frankly triumphant, and I think: "That's got to be it."

It's positively operatic.

Certain Poems
Quoted in the Saga

vividly from her childhood in the
Land when Crevn con-
as they rode toward Roniah, the

Certain Poems
Quoted in the Saga

READERS MAY BE CURIOUS about three poems referred to or quoted in the Saga.

The first is "There Was Once a Puffin," which the author remembers most vividly from her childhood in the 1930s. In *The Many-Colored Land*, when Creyn conversed with Elizabeth as they rode toward Roniah, the Tanu redactor twitted the human woman gently and urged her not to scorn the proffered friendship of the exotic race—who were operants like herself, if only imperfect ones. He paraphrased the poem, which he claims to have learned from "a human educator, long deceased."

THERE WAS ONCE A PUFFIN

by Florence Page Jaques

Oh, there was once a Puffin,
Just the shape of a muffin,
And he lived on an island
In the
      bright
         blue sea!

He ate little fishes,
That were most delicious
And he had them for supper
And he had
    them
        for tea.

But this poor little Puffin
He couldn't play nothin',
For he hadn't anybody
To play
    with
        at all.

So he sat on his island,
And he cried for a while, and
He felt very lonely,
And he
    felt
        very small.

Then along came the fishes,
And they said, "If you wishes,
You can have us for playmates,
Instead of
    for
        tea!"

So they now play together
In all sorts of weather
And the Puffin eats pancakes,
Like you and
    like
        me.

The epigraph to *The Adversary* had my own translation of "El Desdichado" excerpts, which provide such eerie clues to Marc's character. The poet, Gérard de Nerval, now almost forgotten, was a quintessential Romantic who suffered attacks of insanity and died a suicide. He wrote the poem in an autobiographical vein while feeling "widowed" after the death of his lover, Jenny Colon. Nerval imagined himself to be the descendant of a noble Aquitainian family whose castle had long ago fallen into ruins. The Freudian implications of the second line were applicable to the poet as well as to Marc. Later lines in the poem evoke Nerval's travels in Italy with another friend.

Here is the entire poem in the original French, with a translation by Geoffrey Wagner.

EL DESDICHADO

by Gérard de Nerval

Je suis le ténébreux, le veuf, l'inconsolé,
Le prince d'Aquitaine à la tour abolie:
Ma seule étoile est mort, et mon luth constellé
Porte le soleil noir de la Mélancolie.

Dans la nuit du tombeau, toi qui m'as consolé,
Rends-moi le Pausilippe et la mer d'Italie,
La fleur qui plaisait tant à mon coeur désolé,
Et la treille où le pampre à la rose s'allie.

Suis-je Amour ou Phébus?... Lusignan ou Biron?
Mon front est rouge encore du baiser de la reine;
J'ai rêvé dans la grotte où nage la sirene...
Et j'ai deux fois vainqueur traversé l'Achéron:
Modulant tour à tour sur la lyre d'Orphée
Les soupirs de la sainte et les cris de la fée.

THE UNFORTUNATE

I am the dark man, the disconsolate widower,
The prince of Aquitania whose tower has been torn
  down:

My sole star is dead, and my constellated lute
Bears the black sun of Melancholia.

In the darkness of my grave, you who have consoled
  me,
Give me back Posilipo and the Italian sea,
The flower so dear to my tormented heart,
And the arbor of vines where the rose twines the
  branch.

Am I Amor or Phoebus? . . . Lusignan or Biron?
My forehead is still red with the kiss of the queen;
In the grotto where the siren swims I have had a
  dream . . .
And twice I have crossed and conquered the Acheron:
On Orpheus' lyre in turn I have sent
The cries of faery and the sighs of a saint.

In his first conversation with Brother Anatoly in *The Adversary*, Marc mocks the old man, saying, "'And even if my troop fell thence vanquished, yet to have attempted a lofty enterprise is still a trophy.'" He quotes from *La Strage degli Innocenti* (The Slaughter of the Innocents) by Giambattista Marino (1569–1625), translated by "R.T." in 1675. Here is the relevant section of the poem in full:

Non sono anco estinti
Gli spiriti in voi di quel valor primiero,
Quando di ferro e d'alte fiamme cinti
Pugnammo già contra il celeste empero.
Fummo, io no'l nego, in quel conflitto vinti:
Pur non mancò virtute al gran pensiero.
Diede che che si fosse a lui vittoria:
Rimase a noi d'invitto ardir la gloria.
E se quindi il mio stuol vinto cadeo,
Il tentar l'alte imprese è pur trofeo.

Not yet is the spirit of that pristine valour
extinct in you, when girt with steel and lofty
    flames
once we fought against the empire of heaven.
We were—that I will not deny—vanquished in that
    conflict:
yet the great intention was not lacking in nobility.
Something or other gave Him victory: to us
    remained
the glory of a dauntless daring.
And even if my troop fell thence vanquished,
yet to have attempted a lofty enterprise is still a
    trophy.

M. TO E. ON DEPARTURE

So here before we leave I give you
This second little twist of gold,
Lately pain-giving, freed now from fire
As you, my love. The gold will bind you fast
If you accept it, as mine bound me to you
At our first work's completion.
I was too distracted then
By that child that was our first born, by our
    consonance,
To see my own dream ending; nor did I know
What fateful impulse made me clasp
The dead gold like a gyve about my wrist
Before I left you. But it burned.
It bound me to you—to all of them so bound us both—
That you cannot refuse me, and them. So yield.
Accept the second golden bracelet. Trust.
See, now a chain connects us
And the mated galaxies
Not in a catenary
But in a circle, world without end,
Ainsi soit-il.

The Pliocene
Wildcat Lives!

The Pliocene Wildcat Lives!

THE ANIMAL I AM FONDEST of in the Pliocene zoo is the miniature wildcat, Felis zitteli, that importuned Claude Majewski in the Vosges woodland and later became the pet of Sister Amerie and Old Man Kawai. The true habits of the fossil beastie are unknown, of course, as is its coloration. I have taken the liberty of attributing to it characteristics of a similar modern animal with which I am very intimately acquainted.

The Pliocene wildcat still lives—and it is the domestic breed known as the Abyssinian.

The Aby *looks* wild. Its build is slender, slinky, low-slung, marvelously graceful. Its face is exquisitely feline: great greenish eyes, a terra-cotta nose, vibrissae spun of the finest white glass, enormous ears reminding one of a fennec or a kit fox. Its pelt is silken thin, as is suitable to a hot-country animal, pale apricot below and "agouti" above, tawny, with a black-tipped tail, a dark spinal stripe, and white about the mouth and chin. The individual guard hairs are ticked—that is, each hair is striped, giving the coat a subtle changeability.

A good deal of nonsense has been written about the Abyssinian cat—claiming it to be the original feline of ancient Egypt, for instance. In fact, the Aby seems to be an artifact of the breeders, possibly descended from large-eared oriental species bred with North African types. Wherever the little cats came from, they look and act as though they are semiferal—while at the same time maintaining an endearingly affectionate manner toward their pet people.

My own Aby, Catamount Princess Dejah, is a fairly typical specimen of the breed who has condescended to make her home with us for nine years. Her body is some 40 cm long and her tail 30 cm. She weighs 2.6 kilos. When she shakes her head, her huge ears flap audibly. In hot weather and when she is in estrus the ears become radiators, pink and flushed with blood. When the environment is cool the ears turn pale and feel chilly. She can detect the minutest sounds—and when strangers approach the house, she growls ferociously. Her disposition is fearless. As a kitten, about the size of the one Claude found and tucked into his pocket, she attacked our astounded 40-kilo dog, who picked up the little rascal by one dainty hind leg to fend her off, just managing to break the fragile skin at the hock. Deej got out of that one with a single stitch.

Deej displays an interesting repertoire of primitive characteristics. She is normally silent, as is fitting for a creature that would haunt rocky regions and seek small, wary prey. She expresses her affection readily with purrs, however, and with kittens she utters a wide variety of birdlike twitters used at no other time. In estrus she yowls loudly, but only for short periods—males no doubt being few and far between, and predators of little cats numerous.

In heat, she is fiercely intolerant of dogs or strange humans, attacking and growling valiantly. With other cats and humans she is meltingly complaisant when the mating urge is upon her; her normally warm and affectionate nature seems to have its thermostat turned up by many degrees—but, oddly enough, she is not so much crude and sexual as she is seductive and bewitching. A "hot" Aby is even more charming than a cool one. We found, to our astonishment, that she would accept a tomcat even when not in estrus. Presumably, a good man is sometimes hard to find in the wilderness, and one must ever be prepared. Following the sterile mating (with an unapproved suitor) she went into a legitimate heat and was extremely reproachful when denied. To underscore the point, she then had a pseudocyesis, or false pregnancy! We concluded that, in the Pliocene, these little cats were rare, hunting in large territories, and when male met female romance must rule—no matter what the calendar said.

The Abyssinian is a keen hunter, lightning-quick on the pounce. Because the animal's teeth are so tiny, we wondered just what they might eat in the wild. Small birds, of course, and insects. But we also were given an insight into an unexpected type of prey when we discovered what Deej most enjoyed pursuing: slender, narrow things. Her joy is chasing shoe laces, belts, ribbons, strings—even the temples of eyeglasses, and pens and pencils. And when she catches such prey, she maneuvers it back in her mouth to the carnassials, the large shearing molars, and gives a powerful *crunch*. Having caught the little "snake," she efficiently breaks its back—then looks smug.

She is an inveterate climber in high places, roosting on bookcases and drapery bars. When we lived in a huge old mock-Tudor house, her delight was to go out my office's third-story window and prowl the steep roof-ridges while I went into cardiac arrest, sure she would fall to her doom. She never did. Her footpads are black and exude moisture. This, I'm convinced, not only gives her purchase (sticky feet being very efficient for rock-climbing) but would also be cooling when one skips over hot stones in arid regions. As a bonus, the footprints would have pheromones in season, attracting potential mates.

With primitive thrift she "buries" unneeded portions

of food—a trait neither of our other two domestic felines bothers with. She will also attempt to bury thrown-up hairballs or other vomited matter—even if the mess was made by another cat—as if she knew that in the wild, such refuse would tend to attract predators to a sick animal. Her "feral" nature is also noticeable in the way she flees pursuers. When chased playfully by one of our other cats, she doesn't streak away or leap, but rather displays a broken-field running technique, jinking and swerving rather in the manner of a fleeing jack rabbit. It would be very appropriate for an animal attempting to elude pursuit on the open desert or savanna.

Finally, Deej also gave us clues about why cats choose to be domesticated. It really has nothing to do with hanging around Pharaoh's granaries hoping for a free lunch among the infesting rodents. What it has to do with is warmth and the relief of loneliness. For unlike so many cats, domestic and wild, the Abyssinian truly seems to *need* its pet human. One can imagine little Felis zitteli, programmed in the course of its evolution to be ultra-affectionate when the rare mate does come along, huddling alone on a chilly night among the rocks, its scantily furred little body shivering, far away from its home burrow. It sees a strange Thing—a fire—and creeps closer. There beside the source of warmth lies a big fur-clad bundle, also far from its home and sans mate, staring gloomily into the flames. The cat approaches—and performs its charming courtship ritual, arching its spine, cocking its head winsomely, curling its tail in a seductive spiral. And all the time fixing those huge-pupiled, limpid eyes on the bemused human. The hunter parts with a fragment of leftover meat. The cat diffidently accepts, but without unseemly greed. It boldly approaches and butts its head against the benefactor's bare torso... and then tries to worm into the blanketing furs as the man strokes its head. The small body is silky, warm, nice to cuddle. The hunter murmurs the Paleolithic equivalent of "What the hell." Man and beastie drift off to sleep as the fire falls to ashes. In the morning, the little cat is gone, but the human grins in reminiscence, and remembers...

Abyssinians love to sleep with their people. They court you and bonk heads at the least provocation, and also touch noses. In these latter days, Pliocene wildcats exhibit a sybaritic fondness for electric blankets; but once, when I was stuck in my snowbound car in South Dakota and it was minus 17 Fahrenheit, Deej did not disdain to creep into my mouton fur coat with me.

And so it may be that Felis zitteli lives, an atavism reintroduced on Earth by a fortuitous roll of the genetic dice, a throwback bred from the rarefied heritage of aristocratic Siamese and back-alley Mediterranean fence prowlers. It would be nice to think that the first domestic cat came to us seeking affection and warmth—instead of a mere meal ticket.

Three Interviews
With Julian May

Pan Books
Interviews Julian May

JULIAN MAY: I'm fifty-one years old, a professional writer
for my entire adult life. Married to the same man for thirty
years. Mother of three grown-up children. I have three
cats that keep the house messed up and a big Japanese
Akita guard dog that goes backpacking with me. I grow
cute little miniature roses. I play pop songs on a mighty
theatre organ and love to go to the opera. I drive a Bronco
four-wheeler. I sew on a 1928-vintage electric sewing machine. I'm a practical, hardheaded pro. I write for money
and make no bones about it. Starving for the sake of art
has never appealed to me. I like to write and I'm good at
it—but it's my profession, not my pastime. Not very fantastic, eh? Wait!

I was the kid who devoured the Lang fairytale books
at the Elmwood Park Public Library back in Illinois. I
also cut out and saved the Buck Rogers comic strips and
had a stack of Wonder Woman comic books a foot high.
In 1947, when I was sixteen, I discovered pulp SF magazines and became hooked.

249

I sold my first piece of writing while I was at college. It was an article on Walt Kelly, the creator of Pogo. My second sale was a piece of genuine science fiction—a fourteen-thousand-word novelette called "Dune Roller." It attracted a lot of attention. It featured a science nobody had ever heard of: ecology. It had a rousing monster hunt and a discreet love interest and a good deal of colorful background material about the Michigan sand dune country. The story was an instant entrée into the tight little world of SF fandom. I met my future husband at an SF convention. We had a lot of fun and went to a lot of other conventions. I wrote one other science fiction story and sold it ... and then I quit the field for twenty-six years.

Why? It was 1953. The fantasy-book market was in its infancy and the genre was still not respectable. If you wanted to earn a living writing SF, you had to be willing to grind out endless stories for the pulp magazines. Only two of them paid as much as three cents a word. The rest ranged down to one-quarter of a cent on publication—*if* the magazine hadn't gone broke by then. Hardcover and paperback sales were almost nonexistent. Of course I quit! I am of Polish descent—and we Polacks are survivors.

I wrote science materials and nonfiction science books for children. Between 1953 and 1957 I churned out some seven thousand encyclopedia articles on science, technology, and natural history. Between 1957 and 1978 I wrote more than two hundred and forty-five nonfiction juvenile books.

Time marched on ... Around 1976 my husband and I went to our first SF convention in more than twenty years. SF conventions in America have elaborate masquerades where the attendees vie to outdo one another in creating fantastic and beautiful costumes. Well, I made a costume, too, on my antique sewing machine: a diamond-studded silver space suit. It was a stunner. I had let my reined-in creativity go wild! Deep inside my giant brain, the fantastic streak that had lain doggo for all those years erupted.

Sane, sensible me was coming down with a full-scale attack of the middle age crazies. A story to go with the diamond-studded suit began to sprout in my mind. I would be sitting there at the electric typewriter, writing something sensible like *Cottontail Rabbit* or *Billie Jean King, Tennis Champion*—and the story would come creeping...

The story grew. It ramified and grew subplots! After a while I made a folder and sheepishly labeled it "The Novel" and stuck it into the bottom drawer of my desk. Over the next two years I put little slips of paper with ideas into it. The folder grew to be four inches thick. All those wild, wild ideas—where did they come from?...I once estimated that I had read or skimmed nearly fifty thousand volumes in the course of researching my nonfiction juvenile books and writing the seven thousand encyclopedia articles. I read very fast and retain quite a lot of the data. And besides the research I *had* to do, there were certain other topics I delved into for the sheer hell of it: mythology and folklore; psychology—especially Carl Jung; geology and paleontology, which I've always adored; sociology and political studies; history—especially English history, since I'm a keen Anglophile. All this material—plus the English thrillers and mysteries that were my favorite light reading—was grist for my "word processor." I have a very good one—compact, low maintenance, dependable. I wear it between my ears.

I kept filling the folder. I was bored with the SF of the late 1970s: one gloom-and-doom vision after another. Who needed it, with the real world in the state it was in? Readers, I felt, were ready for something completely different. I brooded over folkloric themes, the Norse sagas, the Arthurian legend, Irish and Germanic faerie kingdoms, Tolkien and his modern fantasy treatment of classic mythopoeic themes. And the old-fashioned word processor said: time-travel. I took sophisticated humans from a Galactic Milieu through a time-gate and dropped them in the midst of barbarian mind-wars. And it worked. I constructed a multilayered, massive novel with four parts. On the surface, it was a rousing adventure in the colorful Pliocene of western Europe, six million years ago. Below that I could indulge in character creation to my heart's content, archetypal characters full of courage and humor and earthy sex and archaic violence. The result was the Saga of Pliocene Exile.

I no longer write juveniles. They were not what I really loved to do. Fantasy was my first love, and it probably will be my last. But I'll have to get a new costume closet. The one I have now is full.

Pan Books, Ltd., of London publishes the British edition of the Saga of Pliocene Exile. This interview was published in 1982.

CARICATURE OF JULIAN MAY BY LELA DOWLING

Julian May Interview

Q: YOUR PLIOCENE EXILE SAGA is high on both the best-seller and Hugo nomination lists, yet your name isn't that familiar to fantasy and science fiction readers today. You published several works early, I believe, and then nothing for quite a while. How did that happen?

MAY: I began in 1951, with a story, "Dune Roller," for the old *Astounding*. It was the first story I submitted and the first I sold. It was also almost my swan song, though it appeared in seven anthologies, on television, and on the BBC. They made it into an abominable movie, whose name I will never reveal, and if Forry Ackerman tells, the friendship is off! [Laughter.]

I wrote one other story, "Star of Wonder," but it mostly disappeared into limbo. In the fifties I wanted to be a professional writer, earn a living writing, and I did not think you could do it in science fiction. So I went into other forms of writing. First, I wrote articles for a Chicago encyclopedia publisher—there were eight editors, seven guys and me, and nobody wanted to be science editor, so I became science editor by default. I wrote seven thousand articles on all kinds of science, technology, and natural history: everything from atomic energy to zymurgy, that was me. And having the kind of mind I do, a lot of that material is still there.

In 1957 my editor on the encyclopedia let Popular Mechanics Press know that I could do certain boys' books they were contemplating, boys' fiction that combined science with career orientation. It was a goofy idea, something that's hopelessly klutzy now; but in those days it was considered a fairly legitimate way of interesting children in science. So I wrote ten of these books, and then I began selling books to many other publishers—always juveniles and always with a science orientation, but nonfiction. Later, I wrote other types of things: sports books, conventional biographies, a great deal of natural history. I had always loved science, especially earth science. I had been a keen outdoors person in my day. I'm not as active as I used to be—a little creaky for backpacking and canoeing down roaring rivers—but the experience has carried through into my science fiction.

Q: It sounds like it was of use in the Pliocene Saga.

MAY: I do believe my experience in natural history, especially, has helped me make the Pliocene Epoch seem more real. The Pliocene is a very small-time little period between the Miocene, which was very long and hot, and the Pleistocene, which became glacial very quickly. The Pliocene was a kind of vintage season and that's why I chose it. It had a lot of the animals we have today—no dinosaurs, of course, no pterodactyls ripping out of the sky, grabbing people. There is one anachronism I feel I am entitled to: a plesiosaur, still alive, and quite obviously the Loch Ness Monster. It's a long-necked beastie that feeds upon fish, and at this time, for various geological reasons, it's at large in the open Atlantic rather than restricted to very deep lochs where it might have become landlocked, like certain sharks of Nicaragua. I have another anachronism, a titanic crocodilian critter that is referred to as a dragon.

Q: Don't some people still seriously contend that a few survivors of these reptiles might be someplace around?

MAY: Well, if there is a Loch Ness Monster, it's got to be a plesiosaur. There's nothing else it could be. I wrote a book about the Loch Ness Monster because I think children are interested.

Q: Did you do any research specifically to write *The Many-Colored Land*?

MAY: Yes, definitely. First of all, I researched the science fiction field! I had dropped out late in the fifties, when styles of writing began to change. I was not thrilled with the experimentation going on at the time, so I dropped out—as did my husband [Ted Dikty], who had published science fiction long before so-called mainstream publishers began to publish the stuff. We started an editorial and production service, producing book packages—the entire book, from the writing to the bound copies—for small publishers. We became a kind of miniature Lyle Kenyon Engel, with me as the writer and my husband as designer and producer, for specialty children's publishers [who sold their products mostly to schools and libraries].

Q: So your research was into the possibility of the book?

MAY: Yes. I have always loved science fiction. I had been quoted in print as saying I would love to return to science fiction someday. And when Robert Silverberg took my good old "Dune Roller" for an anthology [*Alpha* 7, 1977], I started to research the science fiction publishing field. I am a keen marketing person. I've been in publishing now for more than thirty years, and I like to sell books. A critical success is great, but I like to live, I have certain tastes, I like to travel around, do wild things. Unfortunately this can take money. So, we've always had a hard eye for marketing... I like to sell my books and write books that will sell.

In this case, I felt that science fiction was ready for a new direction. We'd had experimental and "New Wave" books, we'd had dystopias, we'd had anthropological and socioeconomic critiques. I felt we were ready to return to the spirit of the forties and fifties—not the style of writing; it doesn't hold up—but the spirit: a more humanistic, people-oriented rather than idea-oriented fiction.

I began to think of writing a specific novel, as opposed to just getting back into science fiction in general, sometime around 1976 when we happened to go to a convention again, for what reason I don't remember. I think Harlan Ellison said, "Aw, come on," or something. My husband had gone back into science fiction and was publishing research and bibliographic materials, and perhaps that did it.

I made a costume and wore it at the convention. It was a kind of space suit or flyer's suit, all decked with diamonds. They were all over the outfit and it was quite spectacular. I became very fond of this costume, and I was thinking about what kind of a character would wear it. And eventually—this stays in the subconscious if you're of a certain gaudy frame of mind—over the next couple of years I filled up a large folder labeled "The Novel" with all kinds of research material, mostly aimed at a science fiction novel that would be set in a future about 100 years after we had been contacted by a galactic civilization—what I called a Galactic Milieu.

I had originally conceived of reentering science fiction with a future story, not a time-travel story. I studied mythology intensely because I wanted to use archetypal material and folkloric motifs. The reader is almost irresistibly drawn into that kind of story—he can't help himself. People like Doc Smith are lousy with archetypes, and I was a vast admirer of Doc Smith. His work doesn't bear reading by critical people today, but children love it. I wanted to write a kind of intellectualized Doc Smith saga: galactic scope, blood and guts, sex—although Doc couldn't use sex in the early days of science fiction.

Q: He created an intergalactic Victorian society, somebody said . . .

MAY: Yes, he did indeed! But I wanted to use modern novel techniques that would perhaps be most closely analogous to the British thriller, rather than to a stream-of-consciousness novel or *The World According to Garp* or other eccentric novels that could be compared to science fiction.

Q: Ted [Dikty] told me last night that when you came to the actual writing it was almost anticlimactic because everything was planned so well before you began.

MAY: Yes, I had my folder loaded with fascinating information. I had decided not to enter science fiction again with a future novel. The novel I envisioned and eventually outlined completely became three novels [The Galactic Milieu Trilogy], dealing mostly with mental science and the impact of humanity upon a galactic civilization, presuming that human beings had developed metapsychic powers. (I like elegant phrases, so I use "metapsychic," a European term, rather than "psi" or "parapsychology," both American terms.)

But I was afraid that if I wrote these Galactic Milieu novels first, they would be so esoteric they would not appeal to a wide audience. I want to see people who don't read science fiction at all—people who are intelligent and like thrillers—read my stuff. So I decided that rather than begin with the Galactic Milieu and its sophisticated mental functions, which would confuse readers not immersed in science fiction, I would do a contrast story. I would stay on Earth, and yet I would have my characters be time-travelers from the Galactic Milieu. They are people, recognizable as human beings. I deliberately work on their characterization to make them sympathetic, even the villains. They wear tweed jackets and also strange fabrics we've never heard of; but there are enough reference points so you don't feel lost. I think this is important if you're attempting to appeal to the mainstream—not to lose the reader in the first paragraph by flinging twenty-five neologisms at him.

I love science fiction and I want people to read it. The

world is ready for a new romanticism because it's in such cruddy shape. And there *is* an audience out there, ready to leap into science fiction, if it's not turned off.

Q: Characterization seems to be the basic method by which the reader is attracted into your books. You have a wide range of characters introduced in the first volume, and a lot of development of those characters. It's a big cast, but an intimately understood cast. Did you design those people to fit?

MAY: Yes. The characters are designed basically from psychological types that can be identified in mythology and fairy tales as well as many novels. When I study the techniques of constructing novels, I would rather study a play than novels themselves because the dramatic elements are laid out in a more skeletal fashion, and more easily spotted. There are such things as pacing, which almost no science fiction novelist knows beans about. You have minor climaxes, you have major climaxes, you have flow, you give them comedy relief. If you have scenes of great violence, you follow them with a certain tranquility, making the violence even more vivid in the reader's mind.

I am a purple describer. I am adjective-laden. I try to prune them out, but this is part of the romantic tradition, where I essentially belong, and so I try to pace it. The use of character is similar. Characters are plot carriers in my mind. I work out my plot and decide how to use the characters to bring the plot forward. The characters have definite roles to play. I have been criticized because I've got this mixed bag of characters—the Dirty Dozen: a cashiered space captain, an old paleontologist, and so on. But each serves plot functions as well as just inhabiting the story. Old Stein, the giant crust driller, is necessary for the climax of *The Golden Torc*, as is the archetypal character Felice, who becomes the villainess. I tried to portray her sympathetically as well as horribly. And in *The Nonborn King* I introduce another villain that I love. Even my daughter said, "I *like* him." And that's the best kind of villain to have! The faceless kind, mean and merciless, are overused in science fiction—because it doesn't understand evil. Evil comes in many shapes and is always intermixed with good, because that's humanity.

I like my characters to be strange. They are *not* people I have known, by and large. Some of them come from psychiatric casebooks; some of them, like Richard, are derived directly from folklore. (He's the Flying Dutchman, and his motif, the failed man redeemed, is carried out through the love of a woman, although he is destroyed in the process.) The other characters all serve a similar symbolic use, in addition to their plot functions. And believe me, manipulating an enormous cast like that is a challenge.

Q: Do you feel an affinity for Madame Guderian?

MAY: If I'm anybody, I'm Claude. Claude carries the family name. I am originally Polish, an old noble Polish family of screwballs, the types who would be on the horses leading the cavalry into the Panzer Division . . . So if I'm anybody, I'm Claude. He is a romanticist. That's why he is in the Pliocene; he's crazy enough to go. Once he gets there, he is intensely practical, leading others through the Pliocene wilderness; and yet he makes his gestures. The gesture is everything. I make my gestures, too, and maybe these books are it . . .

But, no. The characters are not people I've met, they're more likely to be found in [Bruno] Bettelheim [*The Uses of Enchantment*]. And so I write about a narcissist Trickster, Aiken Drum. And Brian, the lover who is carried away in spite of himself by passion, who comes to a sad end. When you use archetypes, the books are fascinating from a sneaky, parlor psychoanalysis point of view. If I ever ask you which character you like best, be *very* careful which one you pick! [Laughter.]

Q: Does the fact that Jung has used some of these archetypes have any influence on your work?

MAY: Yes. I began with Celtic mythology and progressed into Jung. Many of his students have gone deeply into literary archetypes. There is a little firm down in

Texas, Spring Publishers, that prints stuff by Jungian people who analyze all kinds of things—not only literature but music and pop culture. They've done books on specific archetypes...

Q: And in your books we have variations on these, at least eight or ten...

May: Yes, the main characters are all, in one way, based on psychological types, if not archetypes. We all like to read about strange folks. We're tired of antiheroes and nonentities, and I'm not interested in writing about them. There has been too much written about characters who react to situations around them rather than attempt to act and influence their environment. The antihero is a schmuck, a schlemiel who gets dumped on. Not being of that persuasion myself, I can't identify with characters like that. So even the ones who are most pathetic will still act. Even Stein, who lost his mother in a hideous accident and never recovered, acts in the end in an apocalyptic manner, as a berserker.

Q: How do you feel about the invasion of the [SF] field by academics in the last ten or fifteen years?

May: When I was a very young writer, just after I had sold "Dune Roller," I went to a writers' conference at Notre Dame. Because I had a piece that was actually going to appear in print, my story was read by a distinguished American poet, John Frederick Nims. Mr. Nims analyzed "Dune Roller"—which is essentially a good old monster story—in such a fashion that I didn't know what he was talking about! I only knew I hadn't written that in *my* story, and I was incensed. From that moment on, I had it in for academics...

By George, if that's what they liked to find in stories, I decided I was going to be sure it was there—and that I had it reasonably under control. Most writers put in archetypes and other goodies instinctively, without even thinking about it, if you like, because they pour *themselves* into their fiction. In my novels, the archetypes, the undercurrents, the different levels of meaning are there.

If you're not looking for them, I promise they won't get in the way of the blood and guts and sex and fun. But if you *are* looking, you can find something like six different levels, all deliberately put there. Top level, of course, is the adventure story. And it's amazing how many critics in the field—good old science fiction critics—said that I wrote an old-fashioned adventure story. It makes me feel great! But there are other things as well. So I've had my "revenge" on academics. They can root around and find all the things I hid for their edification and amusement. But more important, I'm here to entertain us all: the guys looking for a good read as well as the academics who like to find strange things hidden away. This time if John Frederick Nims, Lord love him, were to read the thing, he could wallow if he wanted to. But I try to keep those things under control.

I think writers owe it to readers not to play tricks on them or bore them with mannerisms. My style may be purple, but I don't think you could call it manneristic. It's pretty simple. I do use funny words people may never have seen before unless they look in the teeny-weeny print in *Webster's Second*; and I have Houghton Mifflin's most talented copy editor in stitches. But I'm not the only writer doing this. Gene Wolfe does it, and others, such as Brian Aldiss, also glory in oddball words.

Q: Academics love those, too.

MAY: Well, I hope they're in a context where you can easily understand what's going on. It's not fair to throw in a word you have to look up in the dictionary before you can tell what's happening.

Q: I understand you've felt some hostility from the science fiction "community."

MAY: Hostility to my stuff was inevitable on the part of certain readers, fortunately in the minority, and certain writers—maybe *not* in the minority. I had rather surprisingly negative reactions to these novels, especially when *The Many-Colored Land* was nominated for the Hugo. I was accused of hype. Hype to these people is advertising your book. They would, on the one hand, like to be part of so-called mainstream literature; but when mainstream techniques are adapted to promotion of science fiction, they think it reprehensible. But I write to appeal to a wide audience of people who are not science fiction ghetto dwellers, and I write to sell.

Q: Of course, the Pliocene Saga has been marketed by Houghton Mifflin as mainstream literature.

MAY: Yes. In Britain, it's Number Four on the mainstream bestseller list. This also happened with *Helliconia Spring* by Brian Aldiss. Both novels have an orientation that is by no means elitist science fiction. Both can be appreciated by people who have no SF background. Readers are very eager to read romantic literature, and if science fiction writers can find their own voice in this idiom, they will also succeed commercially as well as critically.

Q: Do you think the ghetto, cult attitude [of some SF writers] is self-defeating in this case?

MAY: I believe it's a sign of amateurism, immaturity. There's nothing wrong with advertising books, or sending free review copies to people. Anybody who says it's an unfair influence is a child.

Q: The third volume of the Saga, *The Nonborn King*, is now in the bookstores. Where does the series go from there?

MAY: There are four Pliocene books. *The Many-Colored Land* and *The Golden Torc* were written as a single volume that could be split at the publisher's option. The last two books, *The Nonborn King* and *The Adversary*, will finish the Pliocene Saga in a cyclical plot movement that will bring us back to the future world of the Galactic Milieu. Houghton has just sent me the contracts for the Milieu books.

The first book of the trilogy, *Jack the Bodiless*, develops an extremely talented metapsychic [Jon Remillard]. His book will deal mostly with the rise of the metapsychic human, and the impact of humanity as it interrelates with sophisticated cultures of the Milieu.

Book Two of the trilogy, *Diamond Mask*, harks back to the science fiction costume I mentioned. We see from this woman's point of view how Earth might have colonized other worlds that had already been mapped out for us by the exotics. We're not going to have to search for planets if there are truly other civilizations out there. They not only know we're here, but they also know what worlds will be suitable for our colonies. All we'll have to do is climb into faster-than-light ships and get on with it.

The third book, *Magnificat*, is the story of the Metapsychic Rebellion of A.D. 2083, where humanity, being imperfect, manages to screw up the Galactic Milieu. We were admitted before our "psychosocial maturation." Humanity is potentially the most powerful metapsychic race in the galaxy, but we are also immature in our social relationships. So Book Three will be the great conflict between human elements sympathetic to the Milieu and its philosophy, and those who want humanity to completely dominate the galaxy.

Q: That sounds like quite a commitment to the future of science fiction.

MAY: I write very fast. The first two Pliocene books were produced in sixteen months. I do the research first and I do careful outlines. I do flow charts, I do character relationships. Can this character be plugged in to make this gimmick work? How am I going to dream up a colorful situation to accomplish this action? This is very important. You can't constantly have people sitting down to dinner to get interaction among six characters. If you're a good craftsman, you think up new situations to get them doing their things, and show the reader more of the social setup. I try to make every scene have more than one function.

Q: I was going to ask you about the "return to the series" as a current publishing phenomenon.

MAY: It's the trend. When you live in a society of anxious people, they are reassured by the familiar. When you have visited a fantasy world and you have mapped it in your mind and begin to feel comfortable with it, it's humanly understandable to want to go there again. We've all seen *The Wizard of Oz* eighty-five times, and we'll go back again and again.

People who rant and rave against series are being immature. I have no bone to pick with any writer who continues to write books that are successful. But you jolly well better have a solid story to tell before you begin a series. When one has worked very hard—and I have—to create a plausible world of fancy, I'm not going to throw it away because some critic believes each book should be fresh sprung from the brow of Zeus.

Q: How do you feel about the annual awards given by the fans?

MAY: I'm an old fan. I started reading science fiction back in 1947, and I did publish a fanzine. I started something called Science Fiction International, a group of fans who corresponded and had this little fanzine. We lasted for a couple of years. So if I'm not quite First Fandom, I'm One-and-a-Half. My husband *is* First Fandom, a true dinosaur! But I consider myself as legitimate a fan as anybody, and I also consider myself a professional writer.

I like to go to conventions and I love to attend SF masquerades. I don't enter the contests, but I love to dress up and have people take pictures, and go to the bar and freak out the mundanes [laughter] sipping my strawberry daiquiri dressed as a lady from another galaxy. At Chicon IV I went as Brede Shipspouse, and my twenty-four-year-old daughter Barbara wore the costume of a Tanu lady farsensor, with gorgeous swirling chiffon and jewels. We were quite a pair wandering around the Hyatt Regency. So I *am* a fan, and I know how to think like a fan, and I appreciate any recognition fans give me. I would hope that someday I could win awards given out by fan organizations.

But I'm also sympathetic to academics. I think it's important to us, if we hope to truly "enter the mainstream," to have academic tracks at our conventions, to welcome criticism of science fiction. I also think we should cultivate the media in a sophisticated fashion. Back in 1952 when I was chairman of [the Tenth World SF Convention] Chicon II, it was "Little Green Men Invade Our City." Last year in Denver, it was "Little Green Men Invade Our City"—the same kind of idiotic media coverage. It's important not to treat science fiction as a ghetto group, a little cult, a pseudoreligion. Because, whether we like it or not, science fiction is in the mainstream *already*. They haven't quite grasped it in the field, but it's mainstream and it's going to stay that way.

Q: And you're going to help it stay?

MAY: I hope I can. I'm a mature writer. These are my first novels, but I've been writing for an awfully long time. But no one admires me as a "first novelist." In one way, it's a great compliment; in another, it makes me sort of wistful...

Q: Is your style a reaction to the so-called New Wave?

MAY: No. When I read for entertainment I usually go to British writers of thrillers and mysteries. I'm not reacting against anybody; I would rather be positive. I've been asked about feminism in science fiction, being a female writer with a name not immediately recognizable as feminine (although it was a legitimate feminine name in the Middle Ages, and that's me—a middle-aged female). [Laughter.] In my novels I've tried to portray a world with a positive relationship between the sexes. Sexism is absent. Richard, the starship captain, being the best cook, does the cooking. Felice, being what she is, is the macho man. There are constant conflicts and interrelations and they have nothing to do with contemporary sexism. Too many militant feminist novels either become too strident, or they rehash old attitudes or deliberately emphasize "female macho."

I was never downtrodden; I never had to be liberated. I was very lucky. I have an aggressive personality—God help anybody who gets in my way. In my family I was not discouraged from doing what I wanted. I have a typically female facility with words. I'm good at writing, and that's what I do. But I don't feel I have to be defensive about feminist attitudes. What I have in my favor is positive feminism and mainstream orientation. I'm not here to teach people. There is a philosophical level in my novels, but it's buried so deeply it's almost impossible to find unless you're looking for it.

Q: Don't you think readers absorb the philosophy whether they realize it or not?

MAY: Yes, of course they do. That's why we writers are so sneaky and must be watched with the greatest care! And I'm sure you academics will be doing just that. [Laughter.]

I am an optimist. I don't think we are going to die in a mushroom cloud. I think something great will happen. I don't know if there are flying saucers—if there *are* galactic civilizations they're quite sensible in leaving us alone until we have attained suitable enlightenment. But I *am* an optimist and it shows in my novels. I've been accused of being upbeat. I triumph in being upbeat! I don't know how successful I have been, but it's been a lot of fun.

The interview was conducted by Dr. Robert A. Collins, transcribed by Ann Hitt, and edited by Douglas E. Winter. It was originally published in March 1983, in *Fantasy Newsletter*, © 1983, Florida Atlantic University, Boca Raton, Florida.

An Interview
with Julian May

JULIAN MAY burst on the science fiction scene suddenly, with a single story that made her a writer to watch. The story was "Dune Roller" and it appeared in *Astounding* for December 1951. It has been anthologized numerous times since, most recently in *Science Fiction Masterpieces* (1983), edited by Silverberg and Greenberg.

In 1981 she did it again, with *The Saga of Pliocene Exile*, starting with *The Many-Colored Land*, and following with *The Golden Torc* (1982), *The Nonborn King* (1983), and *The Adversary* (1984). There followed acclaim, award nominations, and even some controversy, when Algis Budrys cited the books as exactly the sort a fan would write.

Julian has been active as a fan in the past. She chaired the 1952 Worldcon. But she has also been writing busily in other areas. *The Many-Colored Land* marks one of the most successful returns in the history of science fiction.

Q: You came on the scene very suddenly, as far as the science fiction world is concerned. What were you doing between your first story in 1951 and the present?

MAY: In 1951 I wrote "Dune Roller" for Campbell. I loved science fiction dearly, and I wrote one other story, which I had not originally intended for publication. It was called "Star of Wonder"; and at Chicon II in 1952, Sam Mines, having read "Dune Roller," asked me if I had anything else. I said, "Yes, but you won't like it, Sam. It's not the kind of story I've seen, especially in your magazine." He bought it. But after that, I did drop out of the field. There are reference books which credit me with Julian Chain's work. But Julian Chain is really a man named Jesse Charney. In the 1950s you couldn't make a living writing science fiction unless you wrote a great volume of work, mostly short pieces for magazines. I am not that sort of writer. I don't write short fiction. Even "Dune Roller" was a kind of condensed novel. So I went into other forms of writing. I wrote some seven thousand encyclopedia articles on science [the Buck Rogers comic strip, technical manuals, and a catechism with a doctor of theology], among other things. About 1957 my husband and I founded a production service for educational publishers ... Today Starmont House [the publishing company of Julian's husband, Ted Dikty] is primarily a publisher of nonfiction about the science fiction field. This is chiefly my husband's operation. We have "his-and-hers" offices in our house. His office is downstairs and consists of all kinds of shipping rooms and an editorial room with a xerox machine and such, and mine is more of a typical author's den upstairs; but we work closely with each other. He acts as my agent but does not publish my books. I'm published by Houghton Mifflin and other companies. From about 1957 to date I have written and published more than two hundred and fifty juvenile books, under my own name and eight pseudonyms. Most of them are called supplementary reading books, and they're used in schools for children who don't like to read. Rather than give them a textbook, teachers give these kids a book called *Meet the Quarterbacks* or *General Custer at Little Big Horn*, or a book on the life of the fox, or whatever topic the child might be interested in. The kid reads it and it can be used as a tool in helping him to learn. This is the kind of material I have written for the past twenty-eight or twenty-nine years. But I didn't forget science fiction. I considered science fiction my first love.

Q: You were a fan for a while before you were a professional writer. Could you say something about your experience in fandom?

MAY: I began reading science fiction in 1947, and shortly thereafter I had a letter published in a letter column—and it was off to the races. I began to correspond with a number of fans all over the world. As it happened, I specialized in people from Canada and England and Australia. I corresponded with fans in the United States also, but since we were an international group, we decided to form a club. It had the great name of Science Fiction International. I edited and published a fanzine called *Interim Newsletter*, which sort of kept on for about two years, even though it was only supposed to be interim. I haven't seen a copy of it in ages. It was just a typical fanzine, but with an international angle. I remember receiving a letter from Dr. David H. Keller at one point, saying fairly tartly, did I realize that the name of our club, Science Fiction International, was fairly close to the Communist *Internationale*? [Laughs.] Later, instead of the voluminous fan correspondence, I turned to writing various things—not science fiction, though. My first published piece of work was on Walt Kelly, the creator of *Pogo*. . . . My second published piece was "Dune Roller." Before the story was published, I went to my first science fiction affair, a Midwestcon. They were then held at Bellefontaine, Ohio, at a creaky old hotel named Beatley's-on-the-Lake. We called it "Beastly's-on-the-Bayou." There I met such figures as the legendary Wilson Tucker, the legendary Bea Mahaffey, the legendary Frank Robinson, and the legendary Darrell C. Richardson. All the good old First Fans were there; and because I had sold a story, that made me one of the gang. I was welcomed. There was also a young science fiction publisher there named Ted Dikty, who did anthologies. When he discovered I had written a story for Campbell, he said, "I'd like to read it, so that I might consider it for my anthology." Little did I know that his publisher's advances had more in mind than mere money! It was one of those fan romances. We have been married for [more than] thirty years . . . I went to New Orleans for the World Convention in 1951, and at that point something snapped. I agreed to be chairman of the Chicago convention, Chicon II, in a weak moment. I think they thought they were getting a front woman, a sweet, amiable little lady who would do all the work and stand there and smile while all sorts of things went on behind the scenes. But instead they got a real live chairman, who at one point fired a few members of the central committee . . . I was very proud of Chicon II. It was the first "big time" convention. It had the largest attendance up to then, an unofficial total of 1400 people. For the first time mainstream publishers who were publishing science fiction came and set up exhibits just as they did for conventions of librarians and booksellers. We had Campbell; we had a Nobel Laureate geneticist, H. J. Muller; we had Hugo Gernsback; we had [E. E.] Doc Smith as Moon Commissioner. Every convention member got a deed to one crater on an enormous eight-foot map my father had put together. At the end of the convention, someone stole the map. I think it was mounted on four-foot panels; how they did it, I have never been able to figure out. [Laughs.] That was my fan career. I went to two more conventions as the wife of Ted Dikty, and then dropped out.

Q: Did you write for any fanzines other than the international one?

MAY: No.

Q: Did you keep up with science fiction during the period in which you were not writing it?

MAY: Up through the late fifties I read a great deal of science fiction and kept in touch with certain friends we had made in the field. Then we became less interested as science fiction seemed to become more experimental and less traditional. I don't read science fiction for intellectual stimulation. To me, SF should not be didactic, but rather a literature of entertainment. On the other hand, I am entertained on many different levels. I have nothing against "New Wave" writing in principle if it is entertaining—if it has a puzzle element, for example, or if it is very innovative in its use of language. But there were certain kinds of SF stories that I felt were just winging it. They were just amorphous experiments that didn't appeal to me. At that time, the great English thriller writers were flourishing, and I very much preferred their style. So for many years, my way of amusing myself with light reading was with the English adventure and mystery novels. If my techniques derive from any popular fiction, probably it's from British thrillers rather than from any science fiction—except possibly the works of Doc Smith. I would consider Smith to be my literary grandfather. He was a dear man and his stories had the kind of immense vision, the sense of scope and fun and adventure that I revel in. Today, Doc Smith's stories can be particularly enjoyed by younger readers. When I began my own SF novels, I thought I'd like to do something in the spirit of Doc Smith— but in the modern idiom, using techniques I had learned after thirty years of professional writing.

Q: Why did you suddenly turn to writing a science fiction novel?

MAY: It was not sudden. I have been quoted in print as far back as 1974 saying that science fiction was my first love and I would someday like to return to it. There were practical considerations in earlier days . . . I was inspired to begin this series of science fiction novels by a costume I wore at a Westercon. I am a great costume freak. I have a 1928 Singer sewing machine that I bought for fourteen dollars in 1953 and have had ever since. All it does is sew in a straight line: a generic sewing machine. I sew my costumes and some mundane clothes on it. The

diamond space suit I wore to Westercon was my original
inspiration. At first I had no notion of writing a novel;
but then, as I was writing my other stuff, I would wonder
what kind of character would wear something like that.
I began to put little bits and pieces into a folder marked
"The Novel." Off and on I'd add research that I'd think
might be useful. Before long the folder was about four
inches thick. By 1978, I had had enough of this, so I
outlined the three novels that I called the Galactic Milieu
Trilogy. These are set about a hundred years in the future.
They are *not* the Pliocene novels, but they were outlined
first. After I'd worked out the future world and discovered
that it was going to deal with metapsychic faculties, I
came to two conclusions. First, writing novels on this
topic would be very difficult, since I'd have to create
plausible characters who used telepathy and other superior mind powers as a matter of everyday occurrence.
Second, not only would these novels be hard to write,
but they might not find as large an audience as some other
kinds of science fiction. Remember, I wanted to be an
entertaining writer. I wanted to give the reader books that
would be fun. For that reason I decided that I would first
do a more simple type of SF book, a time-travel story
using characters from the elaborate future galactic civilization that was already worked out. I would send these
people back to a suitable era in the past, and using certain
elements of myth and folklore that I was fond of, I would
concoct a Saga. Before I began to write the Pliocene Saga,
I had it outlined almost in its entirety—not in fine detail,
but so that I knew all the plot elements. That's the way
I customarily work. If you're writing lots of books, as I
did for so many years, you've got to be disciplined and
keep things organized or you'll go bananas, you won't
meet your deadlines, and then people won't work with
you anymore. So the four books of the Pliocene Saga
were outlined, and I knew all the broad plotting elements.
I wrote both *The Many-Colored Land* and *The Golden
Torc* originally as a single, huge 270,000-word novel that

could be split in two at the publisher's option. This took me sixteen months, which is pretty swift. I do a lot of rewriting and working over of material. But I usually write two or three chapters, then polish them, and *then* go on, so that by the time I'm finished I don't have to begin rewriting at the beginning again, which is very discouraging. I give the final draft a read-through for typos and obvious errors and inconsistencies, then send it out.

Q: Do you ever stray from the outline?

MAY: Certainly, in a minor sense. There are always new ideas that occur to me. I definitely change things. But I never change major plot elements. My way of writing can perhaps be compared to a dramatist's rather than to a typical novelist's. Some writers sit down and just let it all pour out of their subconscious. Some don't even know how their story is going to end. But a dramatist has to think of his audience, and think of the characters as vehicles of plot. He has to think along these lines: "First I'll have a scene of violence and action, and then I'll have a scene with more introspection so that I can get things ready for the next zap!" I do this all the time. I use vulgarity; I use humor; I use erudition—all coming one after another and contrasting with one another. I have wild passages of description and scenes of violent action or oddball sex. I try to pace my novels in addition to plotting them. These are technical elements that are more common in plays—and in screenplays, especially—than in SF novels.

Q: It sounds to me as if, all your other writing habits to the contrary, you are producing exactly the book you want, rather than the book that will make the largest amount of money, or the one that is exactly what the publisher wants. Are you in a sense writing what *you* want first and looking around for a market afterward?

MAY: All the years I was writing children's books, I was writing what other people asked of me—as various as a book about movie monsters or a series about American artists—which would be terribly esoteric and hard

to get across to little kids. I have always had to write
material that others asked me to produce. So *of course*
my science fiction is what I want to do. I write to amuse
myself. I love to read over my own stuff—unlike some
authors who won't do it, or who maybe read it and cringe!
I like my books. My stuff entertains me. I don't cringe
when I reread it—except occasionally. I wish more writers wrote SF like mine. I love action-filled science fiction.
I am a fan! I have been accused of being a fan and I admit
to it.

Q: You are no doubt familiar with the Algis Budrys
review in which he said *The Many-Colored Land* is exactly the sort of thing a fan would write. He seemed to
be ignoring the fact that you had written two hundred
other books.

MAY: Perhaps he didn't know my career as a juvenile
writer. I wouldn't be surprised if he didn't. Almost no
one in science fiction was aware of what I had been doing
before the Pliocene books appeared.... What is a "fannish" writer is a question I think you'll find hard to answer. Does this mean that I write books that appeal to
fans? Does this mean that a "fannish" writer is different
from a "proish" writer? I'm a professional, and I'm keenly
aware of the trends in popular literature. I write not for
the science fiction in-group but for a wide audience—
even for people who think they dislike science fiction but
still like thrillers.

Q: Do you think any of Budrys's comments are valid,
about how your being a fan affected the kind of book you
wrote?

MAY: It was a very long and rambling review, and it
dealt with many different topics, and I think that unless
you were specific and asked about this or that paragraph,
I don't think I could comment on it very intelligently. It's
been a while since I read it. Everyone remembers that he
said, "Julian May is a fan. This is the kind of book a fan
would write." I don't think *I* really understand what he
meant. I remember Algis Budrys from way back in the

fifties. [We are about the same age and] I think he remembered me as a young fan. At an early Philadelphia convention, for example, I got up on the stage and sang comic fannish songs and accompanied myself on the piano. I know he was there and heard me. I think that images like that stay in your mind, just as a parent will remember a child when it is small and see the child in the adult. Perhaps this fan image was so unforgettable that dear A.J. couldn't get me out of his mind. [Laughs.]

Q: One of the things he said was that, had you not been a fan, you would have put all these people in the Pliocene and left them there in a Robinson Crusoe-type adventure, without introducing further elements; but a *fan* would like to have more science-fictional elements piled in. Therefore, because you were a fan, this is what you did.

MAY: Unless Algis Budrys is a mind reader, he doesn't know why I write what I write. I know that I outline the material with great care, and this is the way I have always written. There are considerable science elements in my books which are, for the most part, pretty valid. The fuzzy bits are hard to find. My dynamic-field theory only *seems* far out—the propulsion mechanism for the flying machines, the superluminal starship field, the sigma-field, which is basically your generic force-field—all these are part of the new physics that's coming along now. My earth science is authentic. So is my genetics. What does Budrys mean, I would have written a Robinson Crusoe story? Perhaps *he* would have written a Robinson Crusoe story. But I cannot relate to "this author should have written a story thus and so." I don't think that is fair criticism. A critic should judge a book objectively after reading it. If he would have written it differently—then he should do so.

Q: Of course this is why "A Christmas Carol" is not the *last* time-travel story. You can give the same idea to fifty different writers and get fifty stories, all totally unlike one another.

MAY: If he is also a writer, a critic must be very careful not to project his own writing preferences into his critical review.

Q: Have you ever done any reviewing yourself?

MAY: No, I am not a critic, although I have done considerable research into literary criticism, especially studies of myth, nineteenth-century romanticism, and the psychology of literature.

Q: How do you get along with critics? How has the critical reception been, and does it influence you in any way?

MAY: There have been all kinds of reviews of my stuff, and I would say that by and large they have been favorable. I think a lot of people have recognized what I am trying to do. I have been called a good old-fashioned adventure writer, which makes me very proud. I also find that academics appreciate the material I'm writing. I am very fond of academics, and have tried to include many levels of meaning in my work. I've done this deliberately. I use mythic elements. I use folkloric elements. I use a lot of Jungian psychology. There's cultural anthropology—and politics galore, because I was originally a Chicagoan, and Chicago is the home of dirty politics! I even have some theology hidden under the gore. But I've tried not to let these deeper elements interfere with the general spirit of entertainment. I don't think that any critic would influence me to write differently. If you don't like my style of writing, then by all means read someone else. If you don't like colorful, descriptive writing, or as we sometimes call it, "purple prose," then read someone with a more lean and Spartan style. If you don't like humor in science fiction, if you think science fiction is a topic of high seriousness, then read someone else. I have serious sides to my writing, but they are hardly perceptible to the naked eye.

Q: It strikes me as a little odd, particularly since you write what you do, that you are favorably inclined toward academics. Many writers, particularly the adventure writers, are hostile to them. Why is your perception of academics different?

MAY: Why are the other writers hostile? That's the question. I know that there are people in science fiction who feel threatened by the academics. They feel that academics are invading "their" field and trying to change it or take it over. This is not to be believed. The academics can only do us good, as they make SF more accessible to people. When I was young, science fiction was barely respectable enough to be on the shelves of the public library. Librarians were seriously wondering: Dare we put these science fiction juveniles by Robert Heinlein out, or will the community rise up? To see science fiction discussed seriously in universities, to see scholarly papers written not only on science fiction writing, but on *fandom* as a sociological phenomenon, is marvelous. If I've got a sense of wonder about anything these days, it's that the academics should be so taken with science fiction, and that it should have achieved such respectability. I don't know whether you attended the Academic Track at Chicon IV, but on the blackboard, placed there by a terribly serious academic, was the immortal quote: "Keep science fiction in the gutter where it belongs." Academics are not stuffy. They're great people. There was laughter and fun and ribaldry galore in the Academic Track. Nineteen eighty-two was the first year that there was an Academic Track at a Worldcon, and I'm very proud to say that I helped sponsor it. I consider myself a kind of academic godmother. Their participation is no threat to science fiction; it can do conventions good by maintaining their status as nonprofit organizations. Many academics are also genuine fans. They have read science fiction since they were young. Tom Clareson is a member of First Fandom, for heaven's sake! He edits *Extrapolation*, one of the original academic journals in the fields of science fiction and fantasy and allied reading. There are many other journals of this type, published both here and abroad, that deal with science fiction on an academic level. These don't appeal to all science fiction fans, but there's nothing in them to be afraid of. Antiacademic fans might try reading these journals once in a while. They might find in them some interesting and challenging ideas.

Q: I think the fear a lot of people have is that, like many other types of literature, science fiction will be something kids are forced to read in school, and will therefore learn to hate.

MAY: [Laughs.]

Q: I remember how I was forced to memorize poetry in grade school. Like everyone else, I grew up hating poetry, and didn't go back to it for a decade.

MAY: If any teacher forced me to memorize parts of science fiction novels, I'm afraid I would hate it, too. But that's not the way it works. Usually the science fiction course is an elective in the first place and the students wouldn't be there unless they liked it. Also, it's mostly taught at the high school or college level. By that time you're taking the course you want to take. There's no question of being forced to do anything.

Q: On quite another subject, what do you plan to do after completing the Pliocene books?

MAY: There are only four Pliocene books. Just as the first and second are closely integrated, so are the third and fourth. One critic, after having read and enjoyed *The Golden Torc*, the second and climactic volume of the first pair of books, said, "I don't see how May can top this." Well, stick with me, guys. You ain't seen nothing yet. May knows all kinds of tricks, and May hasn't hardly used them all up. . . . The way the Pliocene Quartet is written, it carries you in a cyclical movement back to the future world I had originally thought of writing about. So you could go from the Pliocene books directly into the upcoming Milieu Trilogy. Or, if you have never read the Pliocene books you could read the Milieu books and see them as a separate element entirely.

The interview was conducted by Darrell Schweitzer and was originally published in *Science Fiction Review*, © 1984.

A Selective
Bibliography

A Selective Bibliography

THIS LISTING WILL SERVE as a partial answer to that question forever asked of writers, Where do you get your ideas? All of these books were used in the researching of the Saga, and most of them are in my own library. That the listing is only partial goes without saying, especially in the Miscellaneous and Psychology sections. This bibliography is intended to serve as a guide for those who might like to delve further into the mythic or metapsychological subjects that helped form a basis for my fiction, or for those who are simply curious about the wilder shores of physics, mental studies, or depth-analysis of myth and symbol.

COSMOLOGY, ONTOLOGY, AND TELEOLOGY

Berkeley, George. *Berkeley's Philosophical Writings*. Collier Books: New York, 1965.

Billingham, John, ed. *Life in the Universe*. MIT Press: Cambridge, Mass., 1981.

Calder, Nigel. *Einstein's Universe*. Viking: New York, 1979.

Capra, Fritjof. *The Tao of Physics*. Shambhala Publications: Berkeley, 1975.

_____. *The Turning Point*. Simon & Schuster: New York, 1982.

Corning, Peter A. *The Synergism Hypothesis*. McGraw-Hill: New York, 1983.

Crick, Francis. *Life Itself*. Simon & Schuster: New York, 1981.

de Lubac, Henri. *The Religion of Teilhard de Chardin*. Wm. Collins: London, 1967.

Dobzhansky, Theodosius. *Genetics of the Evolutionary Process*. Columbia University Press: New York, 1970.

_____. *Mankind Evolving*. Yale University Press: New Haven, Conn., 1962.

Feynman, Richard. *The Character of Physical Law*. MIT Press: Cambridge, Mass., 1965.

Francoeur, Robert. *Evolving World, Converging Man*. Holt, Rinehart & Winston: New York, 1970.

Heisenberg, Werner. *Physics and Philosophy*. Harper: New York, 1958.

Hofstadter, Douglas R. *Gödel, Escher, Bach*. Random House: New York, 1980.

Jaffé, Aniela. *The Myth of Meaning*. Hodder & Stoughton: London, 1970.

Jaki, Stanley L. *The Road of Science and the Ways to God*. University of Chicago Press: Chicago, 1980.

Jastrow, Robert. *The Enchanted Loom—Mind in the Universe*. Simon & Schuster: New York, 1981.

Jung, Carl G., and Wolfgang Pauli. *The Interpretation of Nature and the Psyche*. Bollingen Series LI, Pantheon: New York, 1955.

LeShan, Lawrence, and Henry Margenau. *Einstein's Space and Van Gogh's Sky*. Collier: New York, 1982.

Lukas, Mary, and Ellen Lukas. *Teilhard: A Biography*. McGraw-Hill: New York, 1981.

Murchie, Guy. *The Seven Mysteries of Life*. Houghton Mifflin: Boston, 1978.

Nagel, Ernest. *Teleology Revisited*. Columbia University Press: New York, 1979.

Russell, Peter. *The Global Brain*. Tarcher: Los Angeles, 1983.

Sarfatti, Jack, and Bob Toben. *Space-Time and Beyond*. Dutton: New York, 1975.

Schrödinger, Erwin. *What Is Life? and Mind and Matter*, Cambridge University Press: Cambridge, 1967.

Shklovski, I. S. and Carl Sagan. *Intelligent Life in the Universe*. Dell: New York, 1966.

Talbot, Michael. *Mysticism and the New Physics*. Bantam: New York, 1980.

Teilhard de Chardin, Pierre. *Activation of Energy*. Harcourt Brace Jovanovich: New York, 1971.

_____. *The Divine Milieu*. Harper & Row: New York, 1968.

_____. *The Future of Man*. Harper & Row: New York, 1974.

_____. *The Heart of Matter*. Harcourt Brace Jovanovich: New York, 1978.

_____. *Human Energy*. Harcourt Brace Jovanovich: New York, 1969.

_____. *Hymn of the Universe*. Harper & Row: New York, 1969.

_____. *The Phenomenon of Man*. Harper & Row: New York, 1959.

Van Fraasen, Bas C. *Introduction to the Philosophy of Time and Space*. Random House: New York, 1970.

Von Bertalanffy, Ludwig. *General System Theory*. Braziller: New York, 1969.

Wilbur, Ken, ed. *The Holographic Paradigm*. Shambhala Publications: Boulder, Colo., 1982.

Zukav, Gary. *The Dancing Wu Li Masters*. Morrow: New York, 1979.

HIGHER MENTAL FUNCTIONS AND JUNGIAN PSYCHOLOGY

Assagioli, Roberto. *Psychosynthesis*. Penguin: New York, 1976.

Avens, Robert. *Imagination Is Reality*. Spring: Irving, Texas, 1980.

Becker, Robert O., and Andrew A. Marino. *Electromagnetism and Life*. State University of New York Press: Albany, 1982.

Burr, Harold Saxton. *The Fields of Life*. Ballantine: New York, 1972.

Clift, Wallace B. *Jung and Christianity*. Crossroad: New York, 1983.

Goldberg, B. Z. *The Sacred Fire: A History of Sex in Ritual, Religion and Human Behavior*. Citadel: Secaucus, N.J., 1974.

Grotjahn, Martin. *The Voice of the Symbol*. Dell: New York, 1973.

Harding, M. Esther. *Psychic Energy: Its Source and Its Transformation*. Bollingen Series X, 2nd ed., Princeton University Press: Princeton, N.J., 1973.

Jacobi, Jolande. *The Psychology of C. G. Jung*. Yale University Press: New Haven, Conn., 1973.

Jaynes, Julian. *The Origin of Consciousness in the Breakdown of the Bicameral Mind*. Houghton Mifflin: Boston, 1982.

Jung, Carl G., ed. *Man and His Symbols*. Aldus: London, 1964.

———. *The Collected Works of C. G. Jung*. Bollingen Series XX, Princeton University Press: Princeton, N.J., 1967 *et seq.*; especially the following: Vol. 5, *Symbols of Transformation*; Vol. 6, *Psychological Types*; Vol. 8, *The Structure and Dynamics of the Psyche*; Vol. 9 (I), *The Archetypes and the Collective Unconscious*; Vol. 9 (II), *Aion—Researches into the Phenomenology of the Self*; Vol. 10, *Civilization in Transition*; Vol. 14, *Mysterium Coniunctionis*; Vol. 17, *The Development of Personality*.

Jung, Emma. *Animus and Anima*. Spring: Dallas, Texas, 1981.

Layard, John. *A Celtic Quest—Sexuality and Soul in Individuation*. Spring: Zürich, 1975.

LeShan, Lawrence. *The Medium, the Mystic and the Physicist*. Viking: New York, 1974.

Matson, Wallace I. *Sentience*. University of California Press: Berkeley, 1976.

Mitchell, Edgar D. *Psychic Exploration*. Putnam: New York, 1974.

Medawar, P. B. *The Uniqueness of the Individual*, rev. ed. Dover: New York, 1981.

Moreno, Antonio. *Jung, Gods, and Modern Man*. University of Notre Dame Press: Notre Dame, Ind., 1970.

O'Regan, Brendan. *Psychoenergetic Systems*. Gordon & Breach: London, 1974.

Panati, Charles. *Supersenses*. Anchor/Doubleday: Garden City, New York, 1976.

Penfield, Wilder. *The Mystery of the Mind*. Princeton University Press: Princeton, N.J., 1975.

Philp, H. L. *Jung and the Problem of Evil*. Barrie & Jenkins: New York, 1959.

Pibram, Karl H. *Languages of the Brain*. Prentice-Hall: Englewood Cliffs, N.J., 1971.

Progoff, Ira. *Jung, Synchronicity and Human Destiny*. Dell: New York, 1973.

Stevens, Anthony. *Archetypes*. Quill: New York, 1983.

Tart, Charles T. *PSI*. Dutton: New York, 1977.

_____. *States of Consciousness*. Dutton: New York, 1975.

Van Over, Raymond, ed. *Psychology and Extrasensory Perception*. Signet: New York, 1972.

Von Franz, Marie-Louise. *Puer Aeternus*, 2nd ed. Sigo Press: Santa Monica, Calif., 1981.

White, John, ed. *Frontiers of Consciousness*. Avon: New York, 1975.

Whitmont, Edward C. *The Symbolic Quest*. Princeton University Press: Princeton, N.J., 1978.

MYTH, FOLKLORE, AND FAIRYTALE STUDIES

Arrowsmith, Nancy. *A Field Guide to the Little People*. Hill & Wang: New York, 1977.

Bettelheim, Bruno. *The Uses of Enchantment*. Knopf: New York, 1976.

Briggs, Katharine M. *An Encyclopedia of Fairies*. Pantheon: New York, 1976.

———. *The Fairies in Tradition and Literature*. Routledge & Kegan Paul: London, 1967.

———. *The Vanishing People—Fairy Lore and Legends*. Pantheon: New York, 1978.

Brown, Norman. *Hermes the Thief*. Vintage: New York, 1969.

Campbell, J. F. *The Celtic Dragon Myth*. Newcastle: North Hollywood, Calif., 1981.

Campbell, Joseph. *The Flight of the Wild Gander*. Regnery: Chicago, 1970.

———. *The Hero with a Thousand Faces*. World: New York, 1956.

———. *The Masks of God: Primitive Mythology, Oriental Mythology, Occidental Mythology, Creative Mythology*. Penguin: New York, 1976.

———. *The Mythic Image*. Bollingen Series C, Princeton University Press: Princeton, N.J., 1974.

Chadwick, Nora. *The Celts*. Penguin: New York, 1970.

Duffy, Maureen. *The Erotic World of Faery*. Avon: New York, 1980.

Eliade, Mircea. *Mephistopheles and the Androgyne—Studies in Religious Myth and Symbol*. Sheed & Ward: New York, 1965.

———. *Myth and Reality*. Harper: New York, 1963.

Evans-Wentz, Walter Y. *The Fairy-Faith in Celtic Countries*. University Books: London, 1966.

Fromm, Erich. *The Forgotten Language*. Grove Press: New York, 1982.

Gantz, Jeffrey, trans. *Early Irish Myths and Sagas*. Penguin: New York, 1981.

Gregory, Lady [Augusta]. *Gods and Fighting Men*. Colin Smythe: Gerrards Cross, Bucks., U.K., 1970.

Guggenbühl-Craig, Adolf. *Eros on Crutches*. Spring: Irving, Texas, 1980.

Hillman, James, Karl Kerényi, René Malamud, Murray Stein, David L. Miller, Barbara Kirksey, William Doty, and Chris Downing. *Facing the Gods*. Spring: Irving, Texas, 1980.

Jackson, Kenneth H., trans. *A Celtic Miscellany*. Penguin: New York, 1971.

Jung, C. G., and C. [Karl] Kerényi. *Essays on a Science of Mythology*. Bollingen Series XXII, Princeton University Press: Princeton, N.J., 1963.

Kerényi, Karl. *Athene*. Spring: Zürich, 1978.

———. *Goddesses of Sun and Moon*. Spring: Irving, Texas, 1979.

———. *The Gods of the Greeks*. Thames & Hudson: London, 1951.

———. *Hermes der Seelenführer*. Spring: Zürich, 1944.

Lopez-Pedraza, Rafael. *Hermes and His Children*. Spring: Zurich, 1977.

Lüthi, Max. *Once Upon a Time: On the Nature of Fairy Tales*. Indiana University Press: Bloomington, Ind., 1976.

MacCana, Proinsias. *Celtic Mythology*. Hamlyn: London, 1973.

Murray, Henry A. *Myth and Mythmaking*. Beacon: Boston, 1968.

O'Driscoll, Robert, ed. *The Celtic Consciousness*. Braziller: New York, 1981.

Oinas, Felis J., ed. *Heroic Epic and Saga*. Indiana University Press: Bloomington, Ind., 1978.

Otto, Walter F. *Dionysus*. Spring: Dallas, Texas, 1981.

Radin, Paul. *The Trickster*. Schocken: New York, 1972.

Rees, Alwyn, and Brinley Rees. *Celtic Heritage*. Thames & Hudson: London: 1961.

Roscher, Wilhelm, and James Hillman. *Pan and the Nightmare*. Spring: Irving, Texas, 1979.

Sjoestedt, Marie-Louise. *Gods and Heroes of the Celts*. Turtle Island Foundation: Berkeley, Calif., 1982.

Spence, Lewis. *British Fairy Origins*. Aquarian Press: Weillingborough, Northants, U.K., 1981.

Squire, Charles. *Celtic Myth and Legend*. Newcastle: North Hollywood, Calif., 1975.

Von Franz, Marie-Louise. *Individuation in Fairy Tales*. Spring: Zürich, 1977.

_____. *An Introduction to the Interpretation of Fairytales*. Spring: Irving, Texas, 1978.

_____. *Problems of the Feminine in Fairytales*. Spring: Irving, Texas, 1972.

_____. *Shadow and Evil in Fairytales*. Spring: Irving, Texas, 1980.

MISCELLANEOUS

Debelmas, J. *Géologie de la France*, vols. 1, 2. Doin: Paris, 1974.

Kurtén, Björn. *The Age of Mammals*. Columbia University Press: New York, 1972.

Oberg, James E. *New Earths*. Stackpole: Harrisburg, Penn., 1981.

Pomerol, Charles. *The Cenozoic Era*. Ellis Horwood: Chichester, U.K., 1982.

Romer, Alfred S. *Notes and Comments on Vertebrate Paleontology*. University of Chicago Press: Chicago, 1968.

_____. *Vertebrate Paleontology*, 3rd ed. University of Chicago Press: Chicago, 1966.

Rutten, M. G. *Geology of Western Europe*. Elsevier: New York, 1969.

Théobald, N., and A. Gama. *Stratigraphie, éléments de géologie historique*. Doin: Paris, 1969.